GREAT LIES WE LIVE BY

i
am stupid
can't swim
can't juggle
can't run
can't ride a bike
can't spell
have no talent
have a lousy memory
am too old
it's too hard to learn

Dr. Stephanie Burns

Second edition
2000

Stephanie Burns

To my father

John Christopher Burns

1933-1977

I am still learning from you

Published by Navybridge Pty Limited

Produced in Australia by Navybridge Pty Limited
P.O. Box 3089
Dural, NSW 2158

For ordering information please write to
info@stephanieburns.com

To learn more about Stephanie Burns and
free access to numerous articles, visit
www.stephanieburns.com

National Library of Australia Cataloguing-in-Publication Data

Burns, Stephanie
    Great Lies We Live By

    ISBN 0 646 13817 0
    1. Learning. 2. Learning, Psychology of. 3. Study, Method of.
    I. Title

    370.1523

Stephanie Burns

FORWARD TO THE SECOND EDITION

Great Lies We Live By was written in 1993 in response to the requests from thousands of graduates of my Learning To Learn and Discovery Camp programs. Those students wished for a means to recapture the lessons and their experiences in those programs.

The launch of the book coincided with my decision in 1994 to end my time as the facilitator for these types of programs. Teaching more than 200 days each year was preventing me from continuing with my research into learning, motivation and communication. In June of 1994 I taught my last class in Sydney, Australia.

At that time I continued to teach corporate trainers, managers and teachers via the Training To Train program. With my new found time I took that program to new cities and returned to school. In 1999 I completed my PhD in Education and after reading this book you will know truly the accomplishment of that achievement. The results of my research are now brought to life in The Labyrinth – Self-Leadership on-line course. I also used this time to write another book, Artistry in Training.

In 1999 I launched an Internet newsletter which eventually matured into an full fledged on-line learning site. This led to an interesting development. That instigated renewed interest in Great Lies for a whole new audience. It also meant that my students from the days of Discovery and Learning To Learn had a means to reconnect with me. They taught me how important this book could be to others. These events combined to inspirate me to revisit Great Lies. I was pleasantly surprised to find that it remains resilient and as useful to the community today as it was when first published. It is truly a foundational piece.

Structural changes have been made to the text, but I resisted editing or changing the contents. It now flows better for the reader, and in doing so makes a stronger impact than did the first edition.

For the past several years I have been working on a teaching model for technology-based courses. That teaching model, having shown great merit, has been applied to most of my original course material. It is also being applied by other content experts as they bring their work to the Internet. There are several on-line courses that are as vibrant as any live training I ever produced. Even the quality of learning has been enhanced. How about that!?

I still reside in Sydney, but no longer on the harbour. I am entrenched in a rural setting with acres, horses and very different life style. I am fully captivated by the work of Pat and Linda Parelli and you will see new work emerging from me as a result of that association.

I am still doing much of I seem to always be doing. Researching, writing, designing and teaching. There is more now than ever available to you. Most of it freely via the website. Please visit me in my virtual office. It is very similar to one I am sitting in right now as I write this. The address is easy www.stephanieburns.com

What I create is there for you to use to enable you to do more of what it is you want to do. Use it well. Learn and Enjoy.

Dr. Stephanie Burns

November 2003

ACKNOWLEDGEMENTS

If there has ever been a life full of influential people, it has surely been mine. I have been blessed with people who have given their time to educate, inspire and motivate. What I have accomplished could not have been done in isolation, and in many cases others have worked harder than I did, which I received the applause on stage.

As I sit down to think about all those who deserve thanks for their assistance in bringing my work to the world, the list grows to a book in itself. I would like to thank everyone who took the time to educate me all those years ago – I have used those lessons wisely.

In relation to the work that enabled this book I owe thanks to the first gang of teachers at SuperCamp. This is still today a thriving business and outstanding resource for parents, teens and teachers. They have done far more than I will ever do in support of helping people learning how to learn. Also, Marshal Thurber and Larry Wilson who put my work in front of some very important people. You boosted my credibility in ways I took great advantage of in the pursuit of helping others. Both of your voices are still very clear in my ear.

Learning To Learn as a course owed its existence to the promoters, their staff and hundreds of production workers throughout Australia and New Zealand. These people supported me nearly every weekend of the year to see that my work reached teachers, parents and members of the corporate community. A special thanks to PJ Johnston and Suzi Dafnis who made it bigger than it would have otherwise been, and for all the real laughs during our years working together. To Diane McCann, James Caldwell and Liana DiStefano without whom there would have been no first steps. And never to be forgotten, thank you Jann Hing for the years of personal care and support of our teams. People learned far more because of your presence.

Stephanie Burns

TABLE OF CONTENTS

Introduction 1

The Great Lies

Lie #1 I am stupid.. 9
Lie #2 I am a failure.. 10
Lie #3 I need talent.. 13
Lie #4 Learning just happens 16
Lie #5 I am not bothered by what other people think.............. 19
Lie #6 Concentrating on mistakes is how you learn............. 25
Lie #7 We all learn the same way............................... 32

The Essential Lessons

Lesson #1   You always were okay 40
Lesson #2   Choosing the right path 45
Lesson #3   What you think is what you'll get.............. 47
Lesson #4   Beliefs are a choice.................................. 54
Lesson #5   Learning finer levels of distinctions 61
Lesson #6   How to eat an elephant 62
Lesson #7   Feelings are not facts 67
Lesson #8   If you can't remember it, you didn't learn it.............. 70
Lesson #9   The art of taking notes............................ 78
Lesson #10 The importance of words 80
Lesson #11 Being great is a choice............................ 83

Conclusion

So what? 84

Stephanie Burns

Introduction

"Human history becomes more and more a race between education and catastrophe."

H G Wells

I have been on stage for nearly twenty years teaching audiences of all ages and all backgrounds. Although I started as a computer design engineer and trainer for the U.S. Army, twists of fate have led me to the forefront of the fields of learning theory and learning technology.

I realised very early in my career that my students' results depended more on my ability to be flexible as a trainer than on their intellect. I wasn't educated in traditional teachers college, so I didn't know that some should succeed and others should fail. I expected all of my students would learn – and they did. If a student was having difficulty, I naturally looked to myself as the source of their confusion. Having expected to find the trouble there, that's where it was found.

My own experience of school was a mixture of ups and downs. I had teachers I liked and subjects in that I performed well, and some I didn't. My experiences seemed similar to those of my friends. We all did well enough to sense we would be promoted at the end of the year. The problems I encountered in school had little to do with the content of my courses, but instead had to do with school's invisible curriculum – the values, beliefs and behaviours of my teachers and fellow students. School experiences, and the people we meet there, play a role in determining how we will later interpret life's experiences. I was unusual in that I did not learn these hidden lessons well. If I had, I do not believe I would have the life I have today.

After twenty years of studying how people learn and teaching thousands of students about learning effectively, I believe most people would benefit from a re-evaluation of what they learned at school.

FOREWORD

"The intellectual equipment needed for the job of the future is an ability to define problems, quickly assimilate relevant data, conceptualise and re-organise the information, make deductive and inductive leaps with it, ask hard questions about it, discuss findings with colleagues, work collaboratively to find solutions and then convince others."

Robert B. Reich

DISPELLING THE LIES

Many of the problems of mass education have been created and perpetuated by century-old myths about learning and the brain. Recent technology has dispelled some of the myths and helped us to construct a new image of the human being as a learning system – but that same technology has created new myths of its own.

In 1983, I made a personal commitment to understanding what could be understood about the process of learning – to find the strategies and beliefs that would support competent, effective learning for 100 per cent of my students, 100 per cent of the time regardless of their educational history, in any given subject. I believe people have been educated to be forgetful about successes and to remember well the failures. My students didn't seem to remember or focus on the ways in which they had succeeded as learners thousands of times over. I wanted to create strategies that made sense, based on these repeated successes.

VOODOO LEARNING

The early 1980's were filled with a tremendous amount of what I call "voodoo learning technology" – quick fixes that turned out to be only as good as the facilitator's ability to get the students to believe in them. Many of these strategies relied on intense activity or such a high degree of environmental support that the average person was unable to maintain the effort after the initial period of hype and enthusiasm. Ultimately, it created just one more barrier for the student to overcome.

I wanted to teach learning strategies that people could deduce for themselves from an evaluation of their own experience and which accurately reflected the emerging map of the human brain. This evaluation of our experience requires that we know where to look for lessons within our experience. Many people have left the Learning To Learn seminar asking "how could I have not seen this before?" The answer – because for the same reasons as we have an extraordinary ability to learn, we have an extraordinary capacity to be blind.

THIS BOOK IS BASED ON MY EXPERIENCE TEACHING THE "LEARNING TO LEARN" PROGRAM

This book is based on the work I did teaching people about learning. In my audience, I may have had 15-year-old street kids and 40-year-old PhD students – there may have been an owner of a small business, the director of a big one, clerks, salespeople, computer engineers, a smattering of teachers, professors and parents. I have even had grand-parents and retired people...

At the end of a weekend seminar, they can all read more words per minute and have better comprehension than when they arrived. They have learned how to juggle and how to make important information memorable.

They have remembered what it was like to be a learner and have discovered the strategies for becoming an effective learner. They have laughed, sung, moved and sighed. They have learned about the untruths they learned in school. Some realise that they have been lied to all along – by parents, teachers and peers. Most go on with a confidence they previously didn't possess, to achieve their goals and dreams.

But, of course, this is not where they begin at the start of the program.

UNDERSTANDING THE SYSTEM

I have written this book for anyone who, by desire or by necessity, is re-entering the world of learning. You might be going back to a formal learning situation at your local university, attending a conference held by your organisation or starting a self-study program at home. You may be studying to improve your existing skills for your job or you may be learning in an entirely new area; it might even be just for fun – a new hobby or the fulfilment of a lifelong dream.

This book is for anyone who is experiencing overload – those who have not seen the top of their desk for years because it is cluttered with paperwork that never gets read. For many, the scales have tipped; some people spend more time acquiring new information than they do using it. This book will give you the strategies for clearing your desk, the ability to remember information and the capacity to find more time to use what you learn.

I hope anyone who has been labelled 'slow', 'lazy' or 'learning disabled' will find inspiration in this book. It is also for anyone who left school believing they have limitations and who find the words "I can't" cropping up all the time. This book will debunk many of the myths surrounding learning disabilities and many of you may discover that those labels should never have been applied to you in the first place.

This is also a book for parents, especially those with children having difficulties at school; perhaps your child has difficulty with basic learning strategies, such as, reading or memorising, or perhaps your child is just unhappy going to school. It will help you to help your child to meet the challenge of school, whether the difficulty is with performance or with attitude.

Lastly, this book is for the teacher who is seeking the means to get the best from their students. For those teachers who may be frustrated or angry about the system, about students or about not being able to motivate students to produce the results they know can be produced. How many of us as teachers have simply forgotten what it is like to be a learner in a classroom situation? I hope this book might recreate a sense of the real value of teaching and put a spark of fun and creativity into your work.

THIS BOOK IS FOR THOSE WHO HAVE LEARNED TO SAY:

- I'm too slow.
- I'm too old.
- It's too late.
- That's too hard.
- There's not enough time.
- I'm a poor reader, reading is boring and I never remember what I read.
- I'm stupid.
- I can't spell and that means that I'm not very smart.
- I have such a poor memory. I'm forgetful.

You were NOT born thinking these thoughts – you learned them. You evaluated events and came to these conclusions. You did not do that on your own. With new information and another way of looking at learning events, your thinking will change. You will find out that there is more than enough time, that you are not too old, and as a functioning human being, it is not likely that you have a poor memory.

STRIKING A NERVE

On 7 March 1992, the Australian magazine "New Idea" ran a short 500-word article on my work, entitled 'Juggling Careers'. You wouldn't think that much could be said in 500 words, but somehow the journalist struck a deep nerve. I received hundreds of letters from readers; they had only two things in common – they were all human and they had all been to school. People wrote about themselves in surprising ways. They recounted stories of their student days and about decisions they had made about their own potential. Some of those statements are worth quoting – perhaps they sound like your story, too.

> *"I want to write poetry... get through this invisible block stopping me from carrying on, ...but it's not worthwhile, nobody would like them, and I feel defeated before I start... makes me feel angry... a long time since speaking to anyone outside my own circle, which is my husband and I, so you can imagine the barriers a person stores in their mind. . . maybe it's the wrong way to think, but until I get your input I'll never know where I am going."*

> *"I was slightly above average at school but (I'm 58 now) have trouble taking things in at times and remembering them now. I must mention that I am in a mentally stressful situation..."*

> *"Could you help me to learn how to learn. All my life I have felt I am a duncehead – I would love to learn to swim and play keyboard and how to study the Bible effectively."*

> *"I agree entirely that schools only really cater to 22% of the population. I am now an ex-teacher because of the frustration I felt in trying to circumvent the institutionalised learning..."*

"... finding it hard to learn new things. I loved reading but don't do it so much any more because I can't concentrate and I keep reading over the same few lines all the time. I can't retain what I learn."

"I sail and I love it, but I won't do it seriously because I can't remember all the nautical terms."

"My youngest son is 11 years old and only last year we found out he had astigmatism after years of being told he was lazy, immature, and stupid."

How is it that we learn to minimise what is possible for us? At what stage, and by whose hand, do we learn to undermine our potential?

Confidence, social skills, good co-ordination, high self-esteem, concentration, energy and health are built on experience. Unfortunately, we have learned to interpret our experiences to produce the opposite effect. Through school, many of us learn useless lessons from our experiences. In this way, people actually learn:

- Poor concentration
- Ineffective reading and memory strategies
- To be depressed
- To talk to themselves in demeaning and demoralising ways
- To develop low self-esteem
- To have low expectations
- To be shy
- To be poorly co-ordinated
- To do things in ways that are fatiguing and perpetuate low energy
- To diminish successes and generalise failures
- To be forgetful

I am anything but antagonistic towards schools. I understand how the school system evolved. I know what it was designed to do, how it succeeded and the stresses it contends with today. I recognise that those who maintain the system are products of the system. There are hard questions to ask, but they are not criticism for the sake of criticism – they are explorations for the future.

Stephanie Burns

YOU HAVE IT ALL ALREADY

Obviously, we have arrived at a critical juncture – a time when mediocre thinking, average performance of skills and basic reading, writing and arithmetic are no longer enough. You know it, I know it, children know it, teachers know it and governments know it.

To meet the challenges of the future, more people will need the opportunity to maximise their potential. The world is on a constantly accelerating cycle of complexity. School not only fails to provide appropriate knowledge and skills for life in a changing world, more importantly, it deadens us as learners.

The good news is that you do not need more resources than you were born with to meet the coming age. You have it all already. It sits between your ears, it is still alive and well and waiting to be stimulated.

YOU KNOW MORE THAN YOU THINK

If you can read this page, then you have learned. If you can tie your shoes, drive a car, run a business, count to one hundred, remember your keys, prepare a meal, recognise a friend's face – you have learned.

You weren't born able to do any of these things. They all required learning. You are alive, well, kicking and surviving simply because you were born with everything you need to succeed as a learner.

Schools were designed to develop a specific type of intelligence. If your strengths were aligned, you were perceived as being smart. But if your strengths lay in some other area, you were perceived as being not so smart.

The development of the industrial age depended on large numbers of people who had mastered simple skills. Schools were designed to see that there were enough people to keep industry going. Most of us, regardless of our instinctive talents, could achieve the minimal skills required to succeed in school.

The world needed millions of people who could:

- READ (kind of);
- WRITE (kind of); and
- do simple MATHS

People also needed to learn to:

- show up on time;
- follow directions and instructions;
- sit still;
- keep their pencils sharpened; and
- keep their mouths shut

Schools have done a wonderful job teaching that.

Now, as we move out of the industrial age, the skills we need are very different. We still need people who can read, write, and do simple maths – but more and more, we will need people who can lead, who can create, who can design, who can teach, who can laugh.

So here's the situation you find yourself in. You came through a school system designed for another age. It couldn't prepare you for the future you wake up to every day. It's time now to re-assess, to dispel the myths, to get back to basics. But the basics are not simply reading, writing and arithmetic. The basics include an understanding of the learning system you were born with and strategies for using that system effectively when sitting down to learn something.

The Great Lies

"Human beings have an amazing ability to learn. The good side to this is that you can learn things exquisitely and rapidly. The bad side is that you can learn garbage just as easily as you can learn useful things."

Richard Bandler

LIE No. 1 – I AM STUPID

"I am entirely certain that twenty years from now we will look back at education as it is practised in most schools today and wonder that we could have tolerated anything so primitive."

John W. Gardner

I won't argue that you can think you're stupid. You might even feel stupid sometimes – but if you look at all you have learned, you can't be stupid.

Our education system, which is a significant source of our thought about ourselves as learners, is based on centuries of theory and speculation about the human brain. What we knew about the brain, when schooling first appeared, was primarily based on dead ones studied during autopsies.

The brain we had at birth is not the brain we have now. Only a relatively small percentage of brain development occurs before birth; the rest happens afterwards. As Robert Ornstein writes, "Because of the long period of infancy, and because of the amazing adaptability of the human brain, with millions of uncommitted cells at birth, the world develops the brain. And because the environment is grossly different for each person, the specific abilities each of us develops differ considerably, even beginning in the womb."

The world we live in changes our brains all the time. While the number of neurons (brain cells) cannot be increased, the connections between them can be strengthened or weakened depending upon how we use our brains, and on the richness of our environment.

The trouble is that many of us stop stimulating our brains. For many, that was long before we left school. We have allowed ourselves to shut down, to become semi-alive. Rather than enjoy continual growth that is the right of everyone, we have closed down. Paradoxically, we have used this incredible device known as the brain to look for evidence that confirms our disbelief in our own abilities.

Anyone who made you believe you could be stupid, didn't have a clue what they were talking about.

LIE No. 2 – I AM A FAILURE

What usually happens in the educational process is that the faculties are dulled, overloaded, stuffed and paralysed, so that by the time most people are mature they have lost their innate capabilities.

R. Buckminster Fuller

Every time I received a failing grade after many hours of study, with no effort by anyone to discover how those errors came about, I was being programmed to believe I could fail. In all my years of teaching, I never could figure out how failing and learning fitted together. If a student failed, it was because of an inadequate method of study or something ineffective in my teaching. But the message from school is clear:

SOME GET A'S AND ARE SMART,
SOME GET F'S AND ARE STUPID.

THEN THERE ARE THE REST OF YOU.

LEARNING TO FAIL; FAILING TO LEARN

We have accepted that it is possible to fail in a learning situation. To me, learning and failing are mutually exclusive. The process of learning incorporates all the steps needed to move from incompetence to competence. When you failed in school there were two paths to explore: your knowledge of learning as a skill and the teachers' competence in developing that skill.

The strangest thing about school is that it is okay to fail some lessons and still pass the course. Does that mean that lesson wasn't important after all? Does it mean that only a percentage of what was taught mattered in the preparation school provides for life? If a test is measuring knowledge or skill, and failure was an option, why is it that failed material was not required to be repeated until we succeeded? What kind of message did you get from that? When we link failure to learning, we short-circuit the process. We start making things up that are not true and begin to say things like: "See, I knew I couldn't do it."

What if, for the moment, we accept this linkage of learning and failure?

Here's a situation: Let's say you go to a computer class. In the first week, the teacher gives you 10 technical computer terms to learn. On Friday, the teacher gives you a test on the words. The night before you sat up and did some studying. Of course, you knew you had to learn the terms so, hopefully, what you did had something to do with that. (If you didn't do anything to study the words I'll talk to you later.)

So you take the test and get 50 per cent wrong and 50 per cent correct. That amounts to a whopping big "F." Lots of red ink; looks like the battlefield after Waterloo. Some people, including YOU, probably think you failed.

WHAT REALLY HAPPENED?

Let's find another perspective. True, you did get 50 per cent wrong. But did you fail? What we do know is that the method you used to learn the words the night before didn't work.

You just learned that:

YOU'VE GOT A LOUSY STRATEGY FOR
LEARNING VOCABULARY WORDS

Next week, you get another list of words. I will bet you your pay cheque that if you go home the night before and do the same kind of studying you did last week, you're going to get the same result-some words will have stuck, others will be lost.

You can only fail if by "failure" you mean that you didn't work out a new way of doing your vocabulary studies. If you do this three weeks in a row, you're crazy, but it's okay because nobody has probably ever mentioned to you that:

IF WHAT YOU'RE DOING DOESN'T WORK,
ABSOLUTELY DO SOMETHING ELSE.

It's not that you can't learn the vocabulary words; it's not that you're a failure; it's simply that you have an ineffective study strategy.

Now, back to your 50 per cent on the vocabulary test. Did you know there are two ways your brain can store and process this result? It's up to you that way you choose to think. You may not have learned that you have a choice, but you do.

Here's one way of looking at that 50 per cent score. If you use the lessons of school and reinforce them, as we often do, then you might say to yourself, "Great dunce, you got five wrong. You failed." Then your brain will seek out and re-run all the emotions, feelings and information associated with being wrong, like depression. From there, you'll say things to yourself like "I'm thick," or "It's just like it was in school, I'll never get it," or "I don't care about some stupid test" or even, "I'm too old to learn new things."

THIS IS DANGEROUS THINKING FOR ANY
DEVELOPING MINDS, BE THEY YOUNG OR OLD.

The habit of noticing how many words we spelt wrong is constantly reinforced. "Hey, how many wrong did you get?" "Seven. How about you, how many wrong?"

If you focus your brain's power on the wrong answers and say things like "How could I be so stupid, how did I get that one wrong?" then that's what you'll learn.

Your brain loves a good question. You've just sent it on a mission. It's going to run around and find all the evidence it can for how you can be so stupid, and it will certainly figure out the strategy you used to miss that one word. It's going to figure out "how to get them wrong." And, because you just gave it a bit of energy and excitement, it will use the same "Get Them Wrong Like This" strategy again next week.

But what if we disconnect the thought of failure from the learning environment?

Here's another way to look at that 50 per cent. You got half of the words right. How did you do that? What did you do differently to remember the words you got right? You must have done something differently – even if you can't figure it out at the moment. If you set your brain to search for how you got 50 per cent right, you will come up with things you can do differently next week. Your brain is very smart. WHAT YOU SEEK IS WHAT YOU'LL FIND.

WARNING: Trying to convince an uninitiated teacher, parent or boss to view 50 per cent on a test as anything other than a failure, is not a smart move.

Sometimes you have to keep your thinking to yourself!

THE LONGEST LIST

You have succeeded far more times than you have failed. Yet, for most people, their list of failures is a lot longer than their list of successes. Why do we remember our failures? Simply because failure is where your brain's attention has been directed for most of your life. You learned to do this. Unlearning this one thing would be worth the price of a hundred learning strategy books.

LIE No. 3 – I NEED TALENT

Where did we ever get this notion? Most of us believe it about something we'd really like to learn to do. You need only to talk to someone who has mastered a skill to realise that talent probably played only a small part in their mastery of the skill. Say to these people that they have a natural talent and they'll probably laugh at you. They have spent countless hours developing their skills. What's the difference between you and them? One big difference is that they did it, and you didn't.

Most of us have looked at someone and thought, "Well, of course they can do that, they're different." What startled me at first was that other people looked at me in that way too. Someone, no doubt, has thought the same of you about some skill you have. Only you know how much work has gone into looking like you've been able to do something that easily from the first time you tried.

STICKY LABELS

There are two important labels we use to describe some people. At the outset, they seem to do no harm – they seem to be merely descriptive. But in reality, their very existence is an obstacle for many of us: TALENT and NATURAL.

Reading is labelled a skill, while art is labelled a talent; look at the result of that belief – most people can read and most people swear by all that's holy that they can't draw. You'll hear people say "Oh, of course she has artistic talent, it's in the genes, her parents were both excellent artists." The other side of this is "Oh, don't expect any artistic talent to come out in you, no-one in our family was ever good at art." By applying the 'talent' label to ourselves or to others, we either accept or reject the possibility that we too may be able to produce good art.

But what if reading were to be labelled a talent? You'd be handed a heap of books and told to go at it. They wouldn't try to teach you how to read because they wouldn't want to interrupt your natural creative reading talent. They'd say "Well, of course he can read, you know, both of his parents were readers."

Of course, if art were labelled as a skill, no-one would assume that you would just pick up a pen and draw; there would be precise, step by step lessons and lots of repetition until you mastered it.

HARD WORK

So many skills are seen as uncommon or extraordinary, simply because of the myth that you've got to have talent. I don't know anyone with a skill who didn't work hard to develop it. And, if I had taken the same steps and done the same hard work, I'd have the same skill too.

I have, fortunately and unfortunately, had both of those labels attached to my behaviour by others seeing me use some skill I possess. I say 'fortunately' because when you are perceived as having talent, people respect you and pay a lot of money for your services. I say 'unfortunately' because I know that anyone could do what I have done if they would do what I do.

I watch people apply the 'talent' and 'natural' labels to prevent themselves from even trying.

THE NERVOUS 'NATURAL'

People have often said that I was born to teach. I'm a natural. Hah! Let me tell you two stories about Stephanie, the Natural Teacher.

I started teaching in 1974 for the U.S. Army. On the first day, I walked into my classroom and turned to face 40 male students. I began stuttering so severely that I had to close my mouth. My legs beneath my skirt were shaking so badly that I ended up with big bruises on the inside of my knees. The only thought that came to my mind was to turn away and go to the blackboard. I thought if I could write my name, it would relieve a bit of the pressure.

So, I slowly made my way to the blackboard, picked up a piece of chalk and lifted it to write my name. However my hand was shaking so badly that the chalk began banging against the board. I was so nervous I couldn't bring my hand down, let alone calm the chalk. The chalk began to crumble and soon it was completely shattered; only my fingers were left smacking the blackboard. To this day, I have absolutely no recollection of how this event resolved itself. Some 'natural!'

THE THINGS BEST FRIENDS SAY

After six years of teaching, I was invited to give a lecture to the Audio Engineering Society. It would be my first attempt at simply lecturing, without teaching, to a large audience; just standing up and talking. I had done a bit of this type of lecturing for small engineering groups and I was receiving good reviews – I thought I was ready for the bigger game.

My best friend at the time had never heard me speak in public, but had heard that I was very good in my training sessions; I invited her to attend. It was the first time I felt confident enough to invite someone I knew into a lecture room to give me feedback. I really believed what I was hearing – that I was getting good at this.

On the night, I was so nervous I could taste fear in my mouth. I stood up and everything that could go wrong did. I stepped on my microphone cord, pulling it from my lapel and then stepped on the microphone itself. I told terrible jokes that embarrassed the audience as much as me. And again, I had violently shaking knees, this time in slacks, with no podium to hide behind. At the end of the lecture no one, not one person applauded. My friend came up and said, "I heard you were good. You're not!" and walked away.

THE HIDDEN PATH

Skills are built in layers over time.

Through reflection, we can see the path we followed in learning to do what we do well. Somehow, when a new skill takes hold, we forget about the process of learning it; we have the feeling of having always been able to do it. If you stop for a moment and remember, you know that isn't true, but believing that it is true obscures the vital fact that acquiring another new skill will mean following a similar path.

Learning is always an active process. You have to do something to make a change – it doesn't just happen. And once you realise that, there's nothing to stop you doing anything that anyone else can do.

LIE No. 4 – LEARNING JUST HAPPENS

Inevitably, when you attend a corporate training session, or a university class, or a seminar, you will approach learning the same way you did when you were at school. If you haven't studied learning as a skill, then you will sit the way you sat, take notes the way you always took notes, read the same way you've always read. If you daydreamed then because of boredom, you'll daydream now. If you avoided asking questions for fear of being humiliated, you will avoid asking questions now. The only change you might notice is that the effect of time and years away from school will, in most cases, have reinforced the negative habits and diminished the positive.

Results, like the grades you received in school, didn't just happen – you did something to produce those grades. If you continually produced the same grades, you now know that whatever it was you were doing, you did it consistently. If what you're doing doesn't work, you will have to do something else. The something else is the addition of new choices.

LEARNING ISN'T FREE. YOU HAVE TO DO SOMETHING.

If I want a student to produce good grades, it is my responsibility to see that the student has the choices for study and learning to produce those grades.

Those choices are skills which must be learned at a later stage, if you didn't accidentally stumble on them in school – and most of us didn't. We're only as good in any situation as the choices we have.

To succeed in any activity is merely a matter of adding choices. Everything you feel you cannot do is simply the absence of a new choice.

JUGGLING CHOICES

When I teach juggling in the Learning To Learn weekend, I am always astonished at how many people have difficulty catching a ball. Most can do it with one ball as all their concentration can be focused on the catching hand. But look out when they are trying with two or three balls.

One man was having a terrible time with this. The balls would go up, land perfectly in position to be caught, yet nine times out of ten they would end up on the floor. He was frustrated and feeling that he'd never be able to complete the juggling exercise. No amount of practice was going to change this skill without looking at how he used his hand when catching.

I observed that when he caught a ball, all five fingers of his catching hand were as if they had been glued together. His hand made the shape of a cup.

So, I added one new choice. I asked him to open his fingers wide and to place his thumb so it was opposite his fingers and catch the ball this way. It would make the hand more sensitive to the weight of the ball and the catch more secure. Within the next few attempts he was juggling like the rest of us.

YOU CAN LEARN ANYTHING

People are always doing things the best way they know how. It's not that they can't perform – they simply may not have a choice available to them to produce a different result. "All people make the best choices, given the choices available to them" is a line I first heard from Eric Jensen, one of the founders of Supercamp in America. It added a new perspective to my map of how people learn. Once I let this simple statement sink in, I was able to see it in operation every time I watched people learning.

As I observed, I would discover things that enhanced people's ability to learn and others that hindered it. I firmly believe that anyone can learn anything. A student's failure is not because of an inability to learn or perform the skill. It's because of my lack of choices about how to teach that particular student that specific skill. I became aware of my ability to observe 'how' they approached the learning of the skill and how to add new choices to that approach. As I became a better teacher, I was constantly adding new things to my range of teaching choices. More of my students succeeded, more often, and with greater ease.

SIMPLY THE BEST

For me, the first step to success in the classroom has been to recognise that students are doing the best they can, given the choices they have for studying and learning. This is an important lesson for my students as well – learning to recognise that their results are based on their actions and to realise that they are doing it the best way they know how. I've seen a lot of students from a lot of backgrounds and most of these students have ineffective strategies, meaning limited choices, for learning. It's easy to understand how students fail. It's much harder trying to understand how a good student picks up successful strategies, because the orthodox curriculum doesn't teach these skills.

It ought to be obvious that a good place to begin would be to compare students who get a lot of D's and F's (on a scale from A to F – A being great, F meaning failure) with students who continually produce A's. Both have some superb strategies for producing these predictable results.

If you got poor grades, you should know now it was simply because no one had taught you the choices of an A student.

If I study how an A student produces A's and teach those same choices to an F student, then I would expect the F student would soon produce A's as well.

That's exactly what I have done.

I have never met a student who wants to fail, but I've met a bunch who do fail. If I approached learning and studying with the same choices they did, I'd fail too. So why don't they do something different? Where do they learn to do those different things? By thinking about it? Out of thin air? Where?

LIE No. 5 – I AM NOT BOTHERED BY WHAT OTHER PEOPLE THINK ABOUT ME

"We may also remember that we became more or less smart depending on our teachers' vision of us, that we learned better when teachers invested themselves in their subjects and expected us to do the same, and that we knew very well when our textbooks and teachers were excluding us."

Gloria Steinem

Expectations. What a subject. First there are other people's expectations of our performance – and then there are our own. You can have all the best strategies for learning, but if poor performance is expected of you, be it generated internally or externally, then that is what you are likely to produce.

When I was at school, I was usually confused. I could rarely figure out what was expected of me. It was like fishing. Some days I caught fish, on other days my line got tangled and had to be cut. Sometimes I inadvertently ate the worm; one day I even hooked myself.

I did the best I could. Sometimes I won the 'great potential' label. Sometimes I got the 'attention seeker' label and sometimes I got no response at all. Some days I won the gold star; others I sat in the corner. I couldn't sort out how my behaviour in the same class brought out such good teaching in Mr. Smith and such bad teaching in Ms. Jones.

It appeared to me that my grades had little to do with what I learned; they seemed to have more to do with how the teacher felt about what I did. I spent a lot of energy trying to figure out how to be the sort of student my teacher would like.

I ended up learning excellent strategies for getting people to like me – but I still can't multiply fractions.

THE GREAT WEATHER BALLOON SCANDAL

I was in the seventh grade – 12 years old; for me, a very grey area in life. I played in the band, I talked too much, I was the class clown, I seemed to do well in my studies and I genuinely liked school. Home was going okay, too. Then there was that one incident. We were given an English assignment. We'd been studying and writing poetry (which

I hated) and were asked to do a project (which I loved) to create an anthology of our poems and others we liked. How I loved that word 'anthology' – it sounded so important.

"What are you doing, Stephanie?" "I'm creating an anthology of poems." It was almost as good as the word 'osmosis' I learned in sixth grade.

We had a week to decide how to display our poems; we were told to be creative, to make our designs big, bright and colourful. We could use what was provided – coloured construction paper, yarn and clippings from magazines – or we could find our own materials.

I started like most. I tried out my calligraphy on a few poems. I burnt edges on the paper to make it look old. I gathered pictures representing the poem. It was all standard seventh-grade creativity straight from the traditional school environment. Then an idea hit.

We were studying weather in science and we had sent up weather balloons with our names and addresses, hoping someone in China would find our balloon and send us a letter. I decided that I would blow up a weather balloon – they were about six feet in diameter write my poems on the balloon, then let the air out. If it worked, my poems would shrivel up with the balloon and I imagined little unreadable blobs until the balloon was inflated.

My parents loved the idea. They encouraged me, bought a balloon, watched me write the poems with a felt tip pen and were as horrified as I was, when all the ink ran together as the air was let out. They helped me find out about pens and ink, and how ink dries on a rubber surface. This is information I still remember to this day. With new equipment, I made another attempt. This time, ooh-la-la, I knew it was great! I could see myself back in class. I laughed to myself over the whole idea of it. It was a winner.

A week later, my classmates and I buzzed with excitement at the end of the project. The day to turn them in was at hand. One by one, students got up to present the teacher with their projects. He looked at each one, gave a nod some times, a frown others and then he faced me.

"Where's your project, Stephanie?" he asked.

"Right here," I said as I slapped the deflated balloon a little too hard on the desk.

MY BUBBLE BURSTS

It's still hard for me to describe his face in that moment, although I can still see it as clear as day and I know a lot about people's faces.

"What is THIS?," he demanded.

"It's my project – you just have to blow it up with your vacuum cleaner and all the poems come to life."

One line sticks to this day: "Well, I expected this from you."

Ah-ha! I had met his expectations! It was just his tone of voice that said I was in big trouble.

I was told, "These continuous attempts to seek attention will result in your failure in life."

I was failed on the project. I was embarrassed in front of my peers. I got sick. I didn't go to school for three days. And then I got smart – I figured the guy was a jerk. It had been a great idea. I didn't learn the lesson he was trying to teach me. Thank God. I was one step closer to becoming Stephanie Burns.

WEEDING OUT WASTE

Knowing what's expected in a learning situation can cut out a lot of wasted energy and time. We often spend a good deal of our energy on unnecessary work. As a teacher, if I tell my students as specifically as I can what I expect of them, I am likely to get it. The students have the benefit of knowing where to direct their effort. It is no fun working hard to please someone or to get a good grade, only to fail because what you did was not what was expected. Expectations should be stated up front.

YOU HAVE A RIGHT TO KNOW!

GETTING A CLEAR SHOT AT THE GOAL

Whether I am working with teens in high school, or with adults at formal university courses, one of the strategies I teach is how to approach a teacher to ask for clarity about goals. I have found that teachers and professors feel good when they know a student intends to do well and to work for it.

I send people back to school to ask for time with their teachers. In these meetings, the students ask "If I want to get an 'A' in this course, what will I need to do?"

One teacher might say, "I want to see good attendance and assignments in on time. If you do that you'll do well in my class."

Another will say, "I want to see initiative."

The student will then have to seek clarification of 'initiative': "What does initiative mean to you? If I were being a model of initiative, how would you know?"

The teacher might say, "It's putting your hand up when I ask a question", or "Initiative is when you come to me of your own accord and ask for extra work", or "I would think you had initiative if I saw you helping other students".

You never know what something like initiative means to another person. I teach students to 'get specific' so that they have a clear outline of what they need to do for that teacher to achieve a good grade.

WHY SHOULD THE EXPECTATIONS OF TEACHERS, PARENTS AND MANAGERS BE KEPT A MYSTERY?

I have had students come back from a meeting with a teacher and tell me the teacher said "That's for you to figure out." How useful is that? The student may now feel the teacher doesn't care. They may feel that nothing they do will get a good mark. They may waste valuable learning time trying to figure the teacher out. The student may never figure out what the teacher wants until it's too late and a potentially excellent student is left to hit or miss. It's a waste of energy – a waste that makes me wish teachers would tell their students at the start of every course what is expected of them if they are to succeed.

Teachers know what they are looking for in the behaviour of their students just as bosses know what they expect from an employee. But they will get better results from everyone if they simply tell us how we can win. It is hard to judge someone's performance when the teacher or the manager has not been clear about expectations. The student who is failing may be working just as hard as everyone else, but will almost certainly be focused on an area not recognised or valued by the teacher. The failing student may have never started to work because he has no 'expectation map' in mind.

THE GOOD, THE BAD AND THE TEACHER

I had a conversation with a teacher who complained that "If I tell my students how to get an A in my classes then they would all get A's".

"Do you have a problem with that?" I asked.

"Yes, it wouldn't be fair."

"What's not fair?"

"I wouldn't know who were the good students and who were the bad."

I asked, "What if they were all good students?"

"They can't be."

"Why not?"

She was adamant. "They just can't be, that's all."

What this teacher needed to learn was that by telling her students what behaviour she values, she is merely giving them all a fair chance to perform to her expectations. She isn't giving them a free ride on learning the content of the course – the student still has to do the work. And some will, and some might not.

By not telling her students what she expects, this teacher is responsible for some students failing because they did not know where best to direct their energy.

If there is no way for a student to 'win' in the classroom, then they should know that. At the very least, they will know where they stand from the start and can adjust their behaviour accordingly.

TRIPPING OVER EXPECTATIONS

Expectations have other downsides. Areas in which expectations fail to support learning are found both in and outside the classroom. They can be externally or internally generated. There are some pitfalls surrounding expectations to be aware of when you set your own personal learning goals.

Expectations are a barrier when they do not match up with reality. If your expectations are unachievable, then you are setting yourself up for a 'quit.' I have seen too many people fail simply because they expected too much too soon. If you have never run even a kilometre, it makes no sense to set a goal to do a marathon – this year.

It is not that the goal is not achievable, it's just that the time-frame is unrealistic. On the other side, if you are 50 years old and you want to be an Olympic skier, you'll almost certainly miss that mark as well. It's not that a goal of skiing at a high level of competence is unachievable – but all the time in the world won't be enough to take you to the unrealistic level of Olympic ability.

A HUNDRED WAYS FROM SUNDAY

You may miss your goal when your resources do not match up with your expectations – things like time, money, equipment and information. You need to carefully assess what's necessary to accomplish your goal as you expect, because there's little you can do if you can't get what you need.

That is not to say that there aren't a hundred ways from Sunday to find what you need if you are totally committed to your goal – necessity is a powerful incentive to find new ways of doing things. I'm simply stating the extreme; for example, if you want to practice the piano for four hours a day and there's no way you can set aside that much time, you may give up altogether rather than find out how to take the most advantage of the time you do have.

Expectations that are too vague leave room for misinterpretation. You run the risk of doing a lot of wrong things that seem right at the time. This is what happened to me in 7th grade with the balloon – I misinterpreted the word 'creative.' I did a lot of work, but because of that misinterpretation it was a lot of wrong work. The right reason got lost in the shuffle.

LIE No. 6 – CONCENTRATE ON YOUR MISTAKES, NOT YOUR ACHIEVEMENTS

"Probably all education is but two things: first the parrying of ignorant children's impetuous assault on the truth; and second, gentle, imperceptible, step-by-step initiation of the humiliated children into the lie."

Franz Kafka

This entire book is intended to be a re-evaluation of the things we came to believe as true at school. But first, you must recognise that it is human nature to act as if our beliefs are the truth, and that lie first and foremost must be laid to rest.

We learned some nasty and useless habits while attending school. As a result we now work too hard for too little gain. If you are to create a set of new strategies for learning, then it is essential that you look at the education system and what you got out of it. We'll look again at the experiences of school and re-think success and failure.

You may discover that becoming an effective learner has more to do with unlearning than with learning itself.

I have identified the beliefs that many adults hang on to from their school days by observing my students' behaviour and analysing the underlying premise that supports and encourages that behaviour. Because I have discovered that a different set of beliefs will produce better results, I use a lot of exercises early in my seminar to help students stumble upon their own set of useless beliefs.

BE AWARE OF HOW YOU LEARN

The exercises and questions I pose are to help my students become consciously aware of "how" they behave in a learning situation. Although their approach feels quite normal and natural to them during the exercises, they are often astonished when it is examined more closely. Here are some examples:

In every Learning To Learn seminar I give my students the following test. The test is designed with numbers in rows across the page. The student's job, I tell them, is to look at the number on the left-hand side of the row and then read the numbers in the row to find the matching number. When they find the matching number they are to put a mark on it with a pen. They are to do this for each row on the test.

When they have found the matching number in each row, they are to look up to me and write down the time I am pointing to on a flip chart. They are told that the goal is to do this as quickly as possible.

Off they go. No one seems to have any difficulty with the exercise – it's very straightforward. Some complete it in a minute while others may take up to three-and-a-half minutes.

INNER CHATTER

The interesting points of the exercise come out in the debriefing afterwards. Many people report that they were just clicking along, finding matching numbers very quickly, when they heard some internal chatter – their beliefs started to bubble to the surface.

"Slow down, you're going too fast."

"It seems too easy, this can't be right."

I didn't tell them to think these thoughts! Where did they learn to think and feel like that? Where did they learn that if it seems easy it can't be right and to run their own interference to slow themselves down?

Some participants admit that even though they found the correct matching number, they still checked all the numbers again to be sure they had them right. Where did they learn to double-check work, even when they already had the correct answer? There they are, in a safe, non-threatening environment. It's a simple exercise and the only requirement is that they do it as quickly as they can. But they tell me they heard a voice inside saying, "You're blowing it."

"She's trying to trick us, there must be some hidden test here." I find it utterly amazing that some students assume I would try to trip them up. Who tripped us up, and for what benefit, when we were learning in the past?

In most seminars there will be a student who clearly feels that they have done the test incorrectly because they finished before the others. The result can be embarrassment and I have noticed the fastest student going back to do the test again. I have also seen students so stressed that when the student sitting next to them finishes they will slow down even more. Listed below are just some of the beliefs and behaviours that are provoked – all learned and consistently reinforced in school:

- Stress is not only acceptable, but is expected in a learning situation.
- You learn to talk to yourself in demeaning and demoralising ways.
- You learn to focus on what is not working.
- You learn to generalise bad experiences.
- You learn to deny good experiences.
- You learn to notice what you're not doing.
- You learn to compare yourself to others at inappropriate times.
- You learn to double-check already successful results.
- You learn to doubt yourself.
- You learn to get embarrassed when you were better than others.
- You learn to change a good working strategy after just one mistake.
- You learn to slow down after making mistakes.
- You learn to believe that learning is supposed to be hard.
- You learn to assume that if it's easy you must be doing something wrong.

That's a tremendous amount of insight from one short test. These are just a handful of the useless, nasty beliefs and attitudes that work against you when you're trying to learn. These same beliefs and attitudes also play a part in other areas of your life, and for the most part, they are useless there, too.

SEEING THE PATTERNS

Recognising and evaluating these beliefs and their subsequent patterns of behaviour frequently can shed light on other choices we might make to produce different results. If students apply this recognition to a test like the one I just described, their scores improve dramatically. With that recognition, and without my having to teach them any new skills they will, later in the program, do a similar test – and the average improvement in speed is over 100 per cent. That is not because they have learned to find matching numbers any faster, but because they enter the test with a more useful set of beliefs and strategies.

Another example that clearly demonstrates the useless beliefs and habits we learned in school comes to light when I ask my adult and teenage students about their spelling ability.

I stand up in the seminar and ask, "For how many of you is poor spelling an issue?" I am forever astounded at the 30 to 40 per cent who raise their hands. And these are successful school students and prosperous adults!

You tell me – how is it that a smart person can go to school and come out not knowing how to do the simplest of things, like spelling? Well, actually they aren't poor spellers at all – they have only come to believe that they are poor spellers!

Further exploration has shown that very few of these people (and in some cases none at all) are poor spellers. They spell 90 per cent or more of all words correctly. If I managed to spell 90 per cent correctly, I'd be jumping up and down in celebration – that's a lot of right answers. But these people have come to believe they are poor spellers. Why?

MISMATCH

Spelling is one of many mismatches I find between belief and performance. What people actually do is contrary to what they came out of school thinking and believing they can do.

Once this is realised, the goal is to turn it around so the thoughts and beliefs accurately reflect what is being done. If this situation reflects your experience, then re-evaluating your experience will surprise you. You are much better than you give yourself credit for.

Here's one more example of how people misinterpret their abilities. So often, people will tell me what a poor memory they have. I have asked for examples and I've heard, "It's like when I borrow something from a friend, I always forget to bring it back."

Asking for further clarification, I've asked, "How do you know you've forgotten?

"I borrowed a book and then promised to bring it back. When I saw my friend the next day, I realised that I had forgotten it. Sometimes I will forget every day for a week and I know I've forgotten because when I see that person I remember that the book is still at home."

Stephanie Burns

Is that a good example of forgetting? No.

Look at it from another perspective. The question is, did you forget the book? The answer is no. You remembered the book. Every time you saw that person's face you remembered the book. Now, it's true that remembering the book at that time isn't useful, but it is not a sign of a bad memory. It's a sign of triggering the memory at an inappropriate time.

Whether the problem is reading, spelling, concentration or co-ordination there are some obvious questions to be asked before any judgment is made or any action is taken. When these situations arose in school, or when they do now later in life, someone should have been asking questions. For example, if you say: "I am a lousy speller" – what does that mean? Does it mean that you can't spell any words correctly? Or only some? Do all the words you spell incorrectly have something in common? Does "I am a lousy speller", arise from the fact that at school you spelt half your weekly spelling words incorrectly?

If that happened, did anyone look at how you spelt the other half correctly? If so, did they help you to isolate the good spelling strategy so that you could generalise it to more words on the list next week?

Almost every day, I hear or read about the failure of the education system to teach our children, anxiety about the influence of poor education on the future of the country, about the ineffectiveness of teachers, or learning disabilities, or student failures. All of these are areas of genuine concern, but the focus is on the problems and there is little attempt to identify the causes.

LOTS OF JOHNNIES

When I hear a line like "Johnny can't read," I ask some simple questions. What does "Johnny can't read" mean? Can Johnny read anything, in any context? Can Johnny recognise the letters of the alphabet or words? Exactly how can't Johnny read?

I have been introduced to a lot of 'Johnnies', mostly by concerned parents. I still have yet to meet a true "Johnny can't read." I look for 'how' Johnny reads in those instances when Johnny 'can' read. If I can learn how Johnny can read in those few instances, I can reinforce Johnny's limited reading strategies and generalise them.

As a teacher, I set out to find one way, any way, that works and build from there. If I start from the premise "Johnny can't read," then both Johnny and I have a problem, because my expectation will affect his performance.

If Johnny can't read because he has been labelled with some learning disability, I'm in luck. Johnny and I now have a good excuse for why he can't read and the burden of trying something new, anything new, is alleviated.

I have found it so easy to offer students a new perspective simply by pointing them in a new direction. It is sometimes hard to realise how well we learned the lesson of not questioning authority. Without the simple skill of asking questions and seeking common-sense answers, we blight our entire lives by clinging to useless beliefs.

- Did anyone notice and point out to you that you have to have a great memory to spell the same words incorrectly the same way every time?

- Did anyone ever tell you that spelling is not a measurement of intelligence, but just a measure of whether or not you have a good spelling strategy?

- Did anyone ever point out to you that many successful people throughout history have been poor spellers?

- Did anyone ever tell you that spelling may well have been important in school (because you were tested), but might not be worth the price of a cup of coffee when you get into a career?

We learned in school that it is okay, even if it was not the truth, to believe you couldn't do something that you clearly could. School rarely points to the learning strategies for the solution. You end up being labelled, making it personal and generalising that label to other areas of your life. In fact, it's just that no one has yet taught you 'how to learn.' Nobody tells us that our behaviour (meaning our actions) can change. I have no recollection of a teacher stopping to check how I was attempting to learn my spelling words, or anything else for that matter.

But I do remember many of the assumptions that were made. I was called 'lazy'. I was told I didn't study when I had studied. I was told I talked too much, although my talking had little or nothing to do with my spelling performance.

THE ANSWERS ARE THERE

If our attention is focused on the problem in this way, it's not surprising that we see no solutions – yet the solutions are there and they're easy. It's not that you can't spell or can't learn. First of all, you can learn and you have learned. You may, or may not, however, have effective spelling strategies or strategies for learning in general.

My aim is to encourage you to seek different lessons from school and ordinary life experiences. With the new insights this will give you, you can change your beliefs – with dramatic effects on the outcome of your next endeavour to learn. Here are just some of the many new insights you can expect:

- You will learn the value of comparison, when it is between your own past and present performance.

- You will learn that there is no value in comparing your performance to anyone else's performance.

- You will learn to take a mistake in your stride, correct it, and move on.

- You will focus on what is working, and what you can do.

- You will learn that double-checking when you already have an answer wastes valuable time.

- You will learn to trust and believe in your own abilities.

CAVEAT ON SPELLING

Was it important to spell well in school? You bet it was. If you didn't stumble upon a good strategy for spelling you were labelled stupid, and you better know that it has had long-term effects on how you learn in general and what you believe about yourself today.

LIE No. 7 – WE ALL LEARN THE SAME WAY

"The truth is that schooling for millions of children ... is bland and boring. If your child sticks out one iota from the norm – in other words, if your child shows his true individual nature – then there is always the danger that he will be discriminated against or stuck with some sort of label and treated like a category instead of a real human being. Our schools have lost the ability to respond to individual differences."

Dr. Thomas Armstrong

Anyone who has more than one child knows that the notion that we all learn in the same way is a crazy one. If different people learn in different ways then why is it that we judge the learning ability of all children based on one standardised method of teaching and of evaluating the success of a student?

Some people thrived in school and they would give up their careers gladly to go back to school. It was the time when they felt they fit best with the program of life.

For others, school had to be survived, often at enormous cost. For some, the cost was conforming – stifling their own nature and personality in the process. For others, it was excelling at other survival skills, such as quitting before the Higher School Certificate, or cheating, or exploiting popularity or sporting skills. And, of course, some didn't survive the experience at all.

Isn't it a shame that so few, those whose learning style matched that of the expectations of the school, ended up feeling good about themselves as learners? You may be one of those or you may be someone who was left on the side of the road.

Much has been written in the last 15 years about the mismatch between teaching and classroom styles and the learning style of children. Although it is more evident today, many of us have suffered the effects of this mismatch as adults. So many of us struggled in school for one very simple reason – our predominant style of learning was different from the teaching style in school.

We know today that there is no single right way to learn. Many students who are not surviving school or have been thrown on the learning disability scrap heap are learners with a different style. As the world changes and we need people with different skills and talents, we may find that in letting these children fall by the wayside, we are throwing away the seeds of tomorrow.

DON'T BELIEVE IN DISABILITY

A book I have highly recommended to parents is 'In Their Own Way', by Thomas Armstrong. A learning disabilities specialist for many years, he quit, saying, "I no longer believed in learning disabilities. " He goes on to say, "This notion of learning disabilities was handicapping all of our children by placing the blame for a child's learning failure on mysterious neurological deficiencies in the brain instead of on much needed reforms in our system of education."

After years of struggling with what he finally saw as the damaging concept of learning disability, he found that the concept of learning differences could provide new and effective solutions.

What keeps the lie of learning disability alive is the lack of knowledge in the mainstream of the educational community about learning styles. In my teaching, I have never met anyone who was a truly disabled learner in the sense that there was no pathway by which the individual could learn – although many carry the label with them when they walk into my seminar.

The trouble created by labelling is manifold, but for my purposes in this book, it is rooted in the persistent beliefs people come to hold about their own ability to learn. Once the label has been slapped on, even the thought of attempting a new challenge is stifled – hence the durability of the lie.

The stories told by learning disability teachers – including Armstrong – can do a lot to help us as adult learners, by identifying the lies we have lived by – lies based on the unspoken lessons of school which stem from a misunderstanding of learning differences.

Here's a collection from Armstrong's book:

- Susan was a first-grader who read the Encyclopedia for recreation. In reading class, she had to patiently submit to a curriculum that included books with titles like ABC and Me and Little Pig. Finally, the teacher asked the class to write a story about Little Pig. Susan wrote: "Little Pig, Little Pig I'll tell you what you can do with Little Pig. You can *take this book and..."*

- *By the age of twelve, Chris was managing two profitable businesses at home and had a one-man art exhibition at his elementary school.*
- *At five, Justin was giving talks on the solar system.*
- *Marc was an eleven-year-old Dungeons and Dragons expert, widely read on the subject. He also created animated movies.*

Susan, and all three boys, were labelled learning disabled by their schools and forced to attend special remedial classes.

There are three major bodies of work we can explore when we discuss learning styles:

- NLP (Neuro Linguistic Programming) discusses, amongst many things, the need for content to be presented in the way we find most congenial to our style. For some, it's visual, for others it's auditory, and still others respond best to kinaesthetics – movement.

- Howard Gardner's work, relied on heavily by Thomas Armstrong, focuses on different types of intelligence. He used a system of seven outlines to assess learning styles and saw that schools had a strong tendency to develop only one. The result is that many of us come to believe we're not made of the right stuff, when the real truth is that we simply are not made of the right stuff to survive in the existing structure of the school.

- Thirdly, there is the work of learning style specialists who look at differences in our learning style based on our predominant modes of perceiving and processing information.

Recognising your learning style not only assists in understanding the perspectives and attitudes about learning you developed in school, but will help you to understand why you are strongly attracted to some activities but shy away from others.

To open up your thinking about the beliefs you now hold about yourself as a learner, I want to give you a short overview of one aspect of Bernice McCarthy's work on learning styles from her book, 4-Mat.

In every training session I conduct, I need only to mention that we are about to do some activity or learn some new way of thinking to provoke a barrage of questions and actions which reveal each student's learning style.

SEEING THE STYLES

Teaching adults in large groups to play the guitar, I witnessed every possible learning style – they flew at me from all directions.

Some learners will play along for a while and then seem to be unable to go further until they stop and write down what they have done. Others stop playing, not to write, but to sit for a while; they appear to daydream, but really they're reflecting on what they've been doing, as if they were trying to categorise the experience.

In breaks, some people cluster in groups and talk about why they had to do the exercises we've just completed; others take their guitars out of the class and try out things I haven't even begun to teach.

Some students won't pick up their guitars until specifically told to do so, and even then they will only play what I tell them to play. No more, no less. They want lots of information and data before playing anything. If I never told them to pick up the guitar, I doubt they would ever feel they knew enough to do even that. Some get their own ideas about how things go together on the guitar and quickly begin playing their own compositions. It's not that they are any brighter than the rest – they just like experimenting with ideas and the result is a good one.

There are some to whom I have to say continually: "Can I please get your hands off the guitar for a moment?" They never stop fiddling with the strings; that's fine if you have only one student – imagine what it's like when there are fifty.

And every class has its creative wonders; if I say an A chord sounds good here, they will play anything but an A chord. It's as if to say, "Okay, I get it – an A chord sounds good here, but what about an F chord?"

If, as the teacher, I believe that a 'good' student is one who pays attention to the instructions first and then does the exercises, then I will see the active experimenters as inattentive, troublemakers, hyperactive, and rebellious.

If my idea of a 'good' student is one who shows initiative and likes to play with the information I give, then I am going to see those sitting waiting for instructions as lazy, slow, unmotivated and dull.

My beliefs as a teacher are coloured by my own learning style – so in both cases, my beliefs about learning will affect my students. I have come to the conclusion that there is no right way, or even a right time, to learn. We all learn in our own way and each way leads to learning down a very different path. Some paths, for some skills, are faster than others. But given the chance, everyone will learn.

Research into learning styles is a great eye-opener. Not only does it help those who haven't been able to figure out why school didn't work for them, but it also benefits teachers working with different learning styles in their classroom. It has helped teachers to reach more of their students, while for parents concerned about their child's behaviour (especially if it seems not to be 'right' for school) it provides some valuable keys to understanding.

IT'S OKAY TO DO IT YOUR WAY

Your learning style is your preferred way of gathering and using information. Schools were designed to teach to those who have one of the four predominant styles of learning. That's great for those who learn that way – but what about the rest of us? If our learning style doesn't match the school's perception of the right way to learn, we quickly learn to blame ourselves, not the school.

There are four major learning styles. In the descriptions below you might be able to identify where you fit:

Style 1. You learn best by experience, as in an exercise or on a field trip, and then sit around to think about it. You prefer to go out and do things and then go inside and mull it over. People who learn in this way ask the question, "Why?" or the other side of the question, "Why not?"

What you are looking for is some personal meaning or relevance for the information and skills you are being taught. You need to know how it fits into life.

Why do I have to mow the lawn?

Why do I have to wear a tie?

Why do I have to go back to university?

Why is this important?

If you are this type of learner, it is futile to say to you "Because I told you so." How many of you heard this when you asked "why do I have to learn algebra?" I asked a teacher about this once and she said, "I teach algebra, but to be honest, I wouldn't have a clue why it's important in life." And then we wonder why 'why' learners don't want to participate!

Style 2. You learn by gathering facts and data and then thinking about them. You want to know the answer to the question "What?"

- What are the facts?
- What do you know that you want me to know?
- What do the experts say?
- What is the most common cause of death among budgies?
- What is the equivalent value of 'X'?

You starve for data to feed your brain. The information you receive creates new information as you connect it to what you already know. You have little need for direct experience, although you may miss out on a lot of life because of it.

You are an observer. You learn by watching, not by doing. You listen to lectures, read books and write good reports. Learners of this kind seem to know what's going on in training sessions because most courses are about facts and data, and this is where they shine. School was designed for this type of learner.

Style 3. You like to learn about what makes things useful – what makes them work. You come up with ideas gathered from information stored in your head or learned in class and then go out to experiment. You'll take apart the toaster or the TV set, build your own barbecues and fix the plumbing. As kids, you mixed ingredients from the kitchen to make volatile cocktails. You are looking for the answer to the question, "How?"

- How does it work?
- How can I use this?
- How does a baby get made?
- How can I apply this new strategy?

Information and skills need to be practical for you. Because you're an experimenter and you learn by getting your hands on things, you usually find that school misses the point. What you learned may not have been taught in a way that showed the practical use of the information.

You are okay at getting the information from the trainer or the book – but when you're not allowed to fiddle around to discover how it works, you get bored. You get up to use the toilet, make excuses to go to the phone, draw diagrams on your notes or make model airplanes. If you're made to sit still, you rock back and forth in your chair and you're the first out of the door for breaks. Conversely, if you are in a 'hands-on' session, you'll be the last to leave; you may even ask if you can come back into the room in your free time to play around some more. If learners of this type survive school, or manage to leave it with their self-esteem intact, they make significant contributions. They are the ones who take new information and make it work in the world.

Style 4. You are the one that school catered for the least and may have damaged most. I know many adults with this learning style who were destroyed by school.

You will usually find the classroom situation intolerable. You learn by experience and experimenting. You like to do things and then you want to know what is possible with what you have learned. You are the learner who loves a field trip to the nuclear power station and wonders what will happen if you push 'that' button. If you are not harmed in school, you can achieve greatness because this is the behaviour of an inventor. You create whole new ways of thinking and doing. The question you need to have answered is, "What if?"

- What if I throw this brick out of the window?
- What if I don't go to school?
- What if I don't eat my green vegetables?
- What if I only eat green vegetables?
- What if I don't wear a tie?

You will do almost anything but what is asked of you. If a spouse says, "I'll know if you take the car because I'll check the mileage," you will say, "What if I drive backwards?"… and then do it. Or if a teacher says, "If you open that jar near your face you'll lose your hair" you will say,

"What if I open the jar near the cat, will it lose its hair?"… and you'll do it. No wonder this type of learner is most often the one put on drugs by counsellors, expelled from school, labelled learning disabled, leaves home for the streets and has purple hair. I say "this" and you say, "Yeah, but what if that?" – and then others around you get annoyed.

However, if channelled, you can "what if" your way to some new way of thinking or doing that will benefit the world.

An optimal learner would be someone with the flexibility to be comfortable in all four learning styles. Our choice of what we will learn is based on our predominant learning style – but that means that we limit ourselves. In some cases, you must have the ability to think things through and generate new ideas. In others, you have to be able to simulate possible solutions in your mind. To find the solution to some problems, you have to jump in and try them out and be comfortable with the risk that you might make mistakes; to be a good skier you have to put on the skis.

WHICH LEARNING STYLE FITS YOU?

You may use any or all of the learning styles at different times and in different situations, but there will likely be one style you prefer. There are tests to help you to identify which is your dominant style. I just want you to know that if you didn't make it in school, it has little to do with your intelligence and a lot to do with your learning style.

The Essential Lessons

"It is a very grave mistake to think that the enjoyment of seeing and searching can be promoted by means of coercion and a sense of duty."

Albert Einstein

If we accept that there were unspoken lessons in school that hindered or blocked our innate ability to learn, then it must follow that there were other lessons missing that could have enhanced that ability. It's time now to look for those lessons and messages.

LESSON No. 1 – YOU ALWAYS WERE OKAY

"It is nothing short of a miracle that the modern methods of instruction have not yet entirely strangled the holy curiosity of inquiry."

Albert Einstein

Most of us carry away from school a single thought which underpins all the myths and unspoken lessons – the thought that our beliefs, or the beliefs of our teachers and our parents, were the truth.

We act, talk, and think as if they were true. If we were to cease to believe this myth, then our natural, inquisitive nature would have busted the other myths long ago. As Anthony Robbins, author of Awaken The Giant Within, says, "The birth of excellence begins with the awareness that our beliefs are a choice."

Many of us fail to learn, or for that matter even to begin to take on a challenge, not because of any inherent lack of intelligence or raw talent, but simply because we do not believe we have the brain-power or skill to do the task. What a waste of our lives when we let our beliefs, which too often have no basis in reality, determine our actions – or our inaction.

The thought that:

- You are too old to learn is a belief, not a truth.
- Success in school equals success in life is a belief, not a truth.
- You have to have talent to play the piano is a belief, not a truth.
- Running is bad for you is a belief, not a truth.

Our education encouraged blind belief in what was taught; the skill of inquiry was sadly missing. We have come to believe that what we see in print is accurate, and that what a teacher or other authority says must be true. We are not encouraged to question the validity of information or ideas. In many cases, questioning amounted to heresy.

THE GREAT ART PENCIL SCANDAL

When I was in third grade I stumbled on a set of art pencils my father used for drawing. Playing with them, I found the soft lead made my handwriting clearer and I liked the intensity of the charcoal colour. I decided to use these pencils for my next homework assignment. I believed the quality of work would show and would be appreciated. It wasn't.

In class a day or two later, I remember the teacher asking in a stern voice, "Who in this room used an art pencil to do their homework?" I froze.

Clearly, this teacher knew it was me, for my name was on the paper. I sat in silence.

"I want the person who used the art pencil to stand up," the teacher yelled.

I could not will myself to move. I looked around at all the other kids, as if I too was curious about who had used the art pencil. This went on for excruciating minutes, when finally my name was called. "Didn't I know that art pencils weren't allowed?" the teacher asked.

When I said, "No, and why not?" feathers flew everywhere. I was brought to the front of the class and humiliated. I was asked to tell the class why I had lied, why I didn't confess, why I was trying to be different. These were not rhetorical questions. I had to stand there and respond! It was a very bad day.

Clearly, the lesson of this event wasn't about the art pencil. The unspoken message was not to question – not to challenge any belief the teacher had, even if it seemed to be a gross injustice.

THE FIRST BIG STEP

Re-evaluating what you have come to believe about yourself and your potential is the first big step. When you review your learning experiences, you may well come to some new conclusions.

- You always were OK
- You have a great memory
- You've been doing it right all along
- You were right – there is more than one way to learn
- You have all the resources you need
- Your successes far outweigh your failures

We develop through stimulation of our senses – stimulation that feeds the brain with information from which it adapts, builds, decides, co-ordinates and grows. You are a human being; you have a magnificently designed mind and body; your brain is more complex than anything in the known universe. You have already succeeded. You were born to learn.

WHAT DID YOU REALLY LEARN IN SCHOOL?

There's no turning back. We live in a very different world from the one our parents and grandparents inhabited. We are inundated with new information; we are the first for whom life-long learning is essential for success. We are the first generation who need to review what and how we learned in school. Depending on your age, your time in school may have been adequate preparation for work, but it is not likely to keep you in a job. You may be of an age, however, in which it is all too clear that school did not, and could not, prepare you for the world we live in now.

INFORMATION OVERLOAD

Information technology has created an information overload that is pushing adults back to school. People need to learn how to learn and how to process and use data more effectively.

A major instigator of change was the introduction of the personal computer by Apple in 1976. By 1981, computers were finding their way into homes, offices and even into schools. It was an exciting time and these small desktop computers were said to be about to revolutionize the western world. Well, they did... and still are, in ever-increasing new ways.

But one revolutionary aspect no one was counting on, nor acknowledging as an important factor, was that to play with the new technology:

ADULTS WOULD HAVE TO GO BACK TO SCHOOL!

No one was prepared for adults re-entering classroom situations in such numbers. Through these adults returning to learning situations, I and other adult educators began to see more clearly the underlying lessons learned while attending school. Most adults didn't have a clue how to be effective learners. For the first time, education became a major theme of discussion at every level of society.

During 1981, I presented seminars to thousands of successful adults:

- Business men and women with high levels of education
- Teachers responsible for educating our children
- Parents of children now in school
- Teenagers nearing the end of high school

You might expect that successful adults going into a classroom to learn a new skill would behave like successful adult learners. They would sit up because they would understand that posture affects performance. They would take notes in a way that stimulates the brain's need for difference and uniqueness. They would ask questions and volunteer answers. They would do their homework! Of course, this is not what I observed. What I saw were adults behaving just like they did when they were children in school. They...

- rocked back in their chairs
- came to class late
- doodled on their papers
- wouldn't ask questions when they were confused
- feared doing anything that might make them look stupid or silly

They volunteered only the information they thought would convince me that they already knew what they wouldn't be able to do. This, of course, was long before they'd even made an attempt and often before I'd even opened my mouth to begin teaching.

SNOWBALLS IN HELL

Teaching is an arduous task when students already believe there isn't a snowball's chance in hell that they'll succeed. Even though adults are successful and competent in many contexts, these competencies did not translate into effectiveness in the classroom. The skills necessary to perform a task are quite different from the strategies for learning a new one. Adult actions in the classroom did far more to inhibit learning than enhance it.

I have to stress here that these people are not just a few exceptions – this was the norm. In an average class of 100 employed, university educated adults:

- The average reading speed will be 200 words per minute. This is very slow.
- The average score on a general comprehension test taken immediately after reading the relevant material will be 70 per cent.
- The notes they take, if any at all, will serve no real purpose, meaning they will never look at them after the class.
- There will be no other strategy than reading one word at a time for locating information in text.
- 40 per cent consider themselves to be poor spellers.
- 70 per cent consider themselves to have bad memories.
- 90 per cent believe they are too uncoordinated to learn to juggle.

In 1981, when I was teaching computer literacy to adults, I had to directly confront the effects of our education system on our abilities and attitudes toward learning. Learning is a skill – but school does little to teach us about using our mental and physical attributes for the purpose of effective learning.

I radically shifted my perspective of people and took a bold step. I began dealing with adults not based on their positions and titles, but based on the fact that they were human beings.

I started to teach people 'how' to learn effectively before I began to teach about computers. It changed their results dramatically – and my life changed forever.

In 1991, ten years later, I was still standing in front of thousands of successful adults – businessmen and women with high levels of education, and teachers responsible for educating our children. They rocked in their chairs, came in late, doodled on their papers, feared asking questions and feared looking stupid.

In all that time, and despite all the new knowledge about how we learn, the situation at large has not changed. Today, still thousands of adults, teachers and parents come to me to learn about learning.

LESSON No. 2 – CHOOSING THE RIGHT PATH

Some people say "How will I understand it unless I try it out?" They need to do or perform actively in order to learn. This is a great approach if you are learning a skill like skiing or playing the piano. These people will learn the fastest way through direct body experience.

Other people need to understand before they try out something new. They say "How can I do it if I don't understand it?" This is a great approach if you're learning to sky-dive or plan to do your own plumbing.

Unfortunately, as with our learning styles, our preferences in this dimension have weaknesses as well as strengths. We will tend to do well in learning situations in which the development of the skill matches our own preferences. But what about when it's reversed? What about those things you want to learn that require the opposite approach?

You may get frustrated and quit before the skill has any chance of taking hold. Or you may never even begin to learn.

LOOK MA, NO HANDS!

Once I had a student who was desperate to learn to play the piano. I asked her what she had already done. She said she had done research on all the best pianos, by reading about them and by asking friends. She bought the best one for her purpose and a pile of self-paced instruction books so she could learn to read music and understand the theory; she had spent months studying them.

I asked, "How is your playing coming along?"

She replied, "Oh, dear, I don't know nearly enough to begin playing yet. I haven't touched the piano."

This woman has a very strong need to understand before she can perform – but all the understanding in the world won't teach her fingers to play. I sent her home to spend one hour per day just making noise on the piano – to bang on it, watch her fingers work, connect the notes on the page to the position of her hands. I set her the task of playing any song she could remember from childhood within a week. And she discovered that one week of performing, of doing, was worth more than all the months of trying to understand.

BY THE BOOK

Another student sent me a memo during one of the Learning to Learn weekends – "Could you please see me during one of the breaks?" "This must be serious," I thought.

When we met he said that he had noticed I was wearing a computerised watch – one that stores phone numbers and memos. He said "I have one just like that, but for the life of me I can't figure out how to get the thing to work."

"What do you mean, you can't get it to work?" I asked.

He said, "I've been able to figure out how to put the time in and work the stop-watch, but not the phone number and memos. I've tried everything. I've hit all the buttons in every sequence I can think of."

"I know it goes through all of that in the instruction book; have you followed the instructions clearly?"

"The instruction book? Oh gosh, I don't think I even have the book. I would have thrown that out. Why would I want to look at the instructions?"

The trouble some people will go to to avoid the path of understanding is astounding. This man spent, who knows how much time, frustrated by being unable to do something that would have been simply solved by a read through the instruction manual.

Neither of these two approaches, one through thinking and the other through doing, is intrinsically good or bad. They both have strengths and weaknesses. It is important to identify which of the two approaches will best move you towards your objective at each step along your path to learning. Almost all skills require a little of both, jumping from one to the other as you move up the levels of competence.

But what if you're stuck on one side of the fence? I am an absolute 'learn by thinking, reading, analysing' type, so I had to commit myself to learning a skill in which I would be forced to perform. It was well outside my comfort zone in the beginning, and it stayed that way for several months. But, as with all new feelings, they neutralised and became comfortable. Since that time, I find I am a much more flexible learner. I'm not averse to trying something out without knowing everything there is to know.

I discovered what a limitation I had imposed on myself; how I wish I'd been encouraged to learn in this style when I was much younger, when I had so many dreams of doing things that turned out to need that type of learning.

LESSON No. 3 – WHAT YOU THINK IS WHAT YOU'LL GET – POSITIVE THOUGHTS GET POSITIVE RESULTS

"Don't find fault, find a remedy"

Henry Ford

I believe the way we talk to ourselves when things happen, during both good and bad events, is the single most significant factor that affects our learning. In many cases in my training sessions, the ONLY thing that determines one person's exceptional results and another's poor or mediocre results, is the expectation each individual has of themself. These expectations can be heard in how they talk and how they explain things to themselves.

At the end of Saturday morning's first session, I pull three juggling balls out of my little blue travel case. I turn to the class with the juggling balls in the air and announce that when we return from the break I will be teaching them to juggle.

It is always amazing to watch people as they return from the break. Their internal dialogue is written all over their face and screaming out of their body language. When they are all seated on the floor, I ask them to tell me the very first thing they said to themselves when I told them they would be learning to juggle.

"You've got to be joking," chimed someone from the back of the room.

"I've tried that in the past and it didn't work."

"Oh, s-!"

"All right, I'll give it a go."

"I can't juggle."

"It'll be fun to try it."

In that moment, I can predict who will learn quickly, who will have fun regardless of the outcome, who will succeed and never acknowledge the accomplishment and who will not make much of an attempt at all – knowing that for them there would be a high price to pay emotionally if they discovered they actually could juggle.

INTERNAL BABBLE

Many people don't take the time to stop and listen to the dialogue they run in their heads; indeed, many people are not even aware of this inner voice. These patterns of language are learned when you are young. Some are made up, based on early experiences and others are learned from listening to the people around you. These internal dialogues replay over and over again. Every change in the day, from running into an acquaintance, to starting a new class, to thinking we need to pick up some groceries, brings on a babble of self-talk. On some days this internal chatter is positive and pushes us smoothly to our goals. On other days it's dreadful – it makes each step hard and long. Sometimes it can stop you moving at all.

When all my other resources are spent, it is my internal self-talk that either gets me where I'm going or gets me to the couch in front of the TV.

THE SCREAMING BULLHORN

My internal dialogue was never more obvious to me than when I first started to train for competing in triathlons.

"You've got to be joking."

With little or no experience, swimming was a major drama. I couldn't swim the length of a 50 metre pool. With water blocking much of the external noise, I was left with a screaming bullhorn in my head. It said nothing encouraging, it talked only of what wasn't working, and this was MY head.

It is most important to recognise that your internal dialogue programs your brain toward success or failure. Your brain doesn't care whether or not you get that promotion, whether you complete that task or whether you ultimately learn to juggle or not. Your brain wants to be right. It will direct your behaviour to match your expectations.

It's important also to take note of what the truth is, and what are merely your beliefs.

Saying that you are un-coordinated is not necessarily the truth – it is simply your belief. But even so, that belief will direct your brain to provide you with evidence of your ability to do uncoordinated actions. I have taught thousands of people who believed they were uncoordinated to juggle. Some will go on to use that as evidence to support future endeavours, while others will go on to say, "Yeah, I can juggle, but I'd never be able to ski." And I throw up my hands in disgust.

YOUR OWN WORST ENEMY

The effects of internal dialogue have been studied for many years. The way we talk to ourselves when things happen can create pessimism, helplessness and depression in some, and optimism and hope in others.

Today we know that pessimists and optimists live very different lives. Pessimists have a greater incidence of ill-health, fail more often in school and suffer more depression. The best book on the subject is Learned Optimism, by Martin Seligman. I highly recommend this book to anyone who finds their self-talk is their own worst enemy.

During one recent juggling session, I observed a woman who continually made negative comments about her performance, even though she was progressing as well as, if not better than some others. One of her achievements was noted by one another student, who made a point of saying to her "I saw you do that – that was great."

Her face turned into a mocking, tight-mouthed grin and she replied, "That was just a fluke, I'll never learn to juggle."

His face turned from a smile to a frown and he walked away with lowered shoulders.

I walked up to this woman and said' "It is your right to talk to yourself as you want all your life, but I would like you to be aware that when you discredit your successes in front of other people, they feel bad."

STEPS TO CHANGING INTERNAL DIALOGUE

Internal dialogue is a learned behaviour. The patterns you have learned can therefore be broken and new ones installed. It is all a matter of becoming aware of the patterns you have and making choices to change them until a new one becomes a habit.

Most negative internal chatter comes from focusing your attention on what isn't working, what you don't know, what you have forgotten.

The first step to changing internal dialogue is to begin noticing what is working, what it is that you are remembering and so on. At the end of a day, people will tell you about all the things that went wrong. Wouldn't it be a good exercise to sit down and list all the things that presented you with opportunities?

Start looking at how many pages you did read from that stack on your desk, as opposed to how many you didn't read. By all means, if you see remembering all those things you've forgotten as evidence of your poor memory, go home and write a list of everything you remembered in the day. The length of that list will astound you. Then start asking your brain how it was able to remember so much, to read so much, to have spotted so many opportunities? Another lesson is important here:

YOU GET WHAT YOU'RE LOOKING FOR.

All of us were born with strengths, and even if our strengths weren't in the domains of language and academic subjects, most of us can read something, spell some words, and write... kind of. It's not what you can't do – it's what you can do, even if it's only at a rather basic level.

Stephanie Burns

It's also about how you do it and what you have been taught to say to yourself when you succeed and when you fail.

SHAKING OFF THE LABELS

We hear so much today about how the education system is failing – how teachers aren't teaching – how students aren't responding. A fundamental premise of my work is that you get what you're looking for. If you want to know how it's not working, you'll find it. Study the handful of teachers who are incompetent and you'll learn a lot about what not to do in the classroom. If you want to find out how a child labelled as dyslexic screws up language, there are lots out there who can show you.

But what if you look for the teachers who, regardless of the mood or behaviour of the class, are reaching every student? There are lots of teachers like this; seeing them in action will reveal some of the differences that make a difference.

What if you studied individuals labelled with dyslexia who have gone on to get university degrees, play professional football or run their own business?

You can find many people like this and learn a lot about new strategies for success, alternative strategies for reading, studying, and surviving the labels slapped on us by teachers, parents, peers and everyone else.

WE ARE TAUGHT TO FOCUS ON WHAT'S NOT WORKING.

Do you remember the weekly history test you had to endure in school? How many of you had the experience of hearing, "All right, Mike, you got six out of ten correct"?

Oh right, and the moon IS made of green cheese.

Your papers weren't even marked that way. The wrong answers were usually marked with big, visually stimulating, highly memorable red crosses emphasising the four wrong answers. Your feelings are dominated by your errors, not by your successes.

"Okay," you say, "that sounds right." Tests are given to point out your mistakes. Your assessment of your performance is based on what you don't know. I hate to say it, but this is just somebody's bright idea that's been passed down through the generations as if it's a universal law.

FOCUS ON YOUR SUCCESSES

There is an equally good reason for noticing what and how you answer correctly.

The way your brain works conditions the way you handle specific experiences in life; and since it's a two-way process it affects the general quality of your experience of life. Some people, at the end of a day, or a month, or even the end of their life, can list all the obstacles that prevented them from getting what they wanted. Others can list all the opportunities. I believe there are equal amounts of obstacles and opportunities in life.

What you remember and hang on to, is simply a matter of what you, or your past conditioning has programmed your brain to seek.

THE GREAT DRILL SERGEANT OBSESSION

I joined the U.S. Army at 18, instead of going to university for my education. At the end of my seven week basic training I knew, without a doubt, that what I wanted, more than anything in the world, was to be a drill sergeant. I knew I had been born to be drill sergeant. What a strange mind I had at 18 years old – but at that age I saw drill sergeants as wonderful human beings; they worked harder than anyone I had ever seen. Looking back, I think the underlying truth was that they had the best uniforms and I wanted to look like that.

The only way you can become a member of this elite corp is to hold the minimum rank of Corporal. I could achieve that rank if I was head of my class at the end of the sixth week and at the end of the course.

I worked hard in my classes, pitting myself against 39 men who all outranked me, were older and had better educations and more life experiences. But, in addition to a capacity for hard work, was the great advantage that for the first time in my life, I was in a learning environment that suited my learning style.

I was head of my class at the end of the sixth week and I graduated in that position too. I had the equivalent rank to Corporal. Unfortunately, although I achieved the needed rank, my request for drill sergeant training was denied; instead, I was told to report for training as a military instructor. That's what they do with everyone who comes top of the class – we're seen as those who are best able to teach future classes.

The internal dialogue kicked in. I cursed everything and everyone in my path. I was devastated to lose my dream and I vowed to do whatever it took to wear that wonderfully smart uniform.

But, after a year of teaching, I realised that I hadn't cheated me after all. My military training has paved the way for all my successes to date and was the true starting point for the work I do today.

I look back now and see I could have been someone who looked for the barriers. If I were, I would perhaps be a bitter person who never took advantage of the opportunity I was given, while I was obsessed by the drill sergeant door that was closed to me so many years before.

ADD APPROPRIATE WORDS TO YOUR INTERNAL DIALOGUE

Another game with internal dialogue is simply learning to add words to your ramblings that keep the door of possibility open. "I haven't been able to get through that book YET," is a lot better than "I'll never get through this book." Or; "When I was younger I was unable to concentrate when reading," is better than, "I can't concentrate."

Here, the door of possibility is open to new and different experiences, and, as you will learn, if you are looking for it, you will find it.

START USING THE PHRASE, "I SIMPLY DON'T KNOW IF I CAN"

Examine your beliefs. They are likely to not be the truth. What would happen if, instead of "I can't," you simply said, "I don't know if I can"? Think of the changes on all levels – motivation, possibility, curiosity – in going from "I'll never be able to complete a triathlon" to "I don't know if I can complete a triathlon." It is simply a better truth. You don't know, you've never tried and the truth is, you really have no way of knowing for sure.

This also goes for anything in which you now recognise that the attempt you made was less than effective. Perhaps you didn't know the effect of your internal dialogue; knowing about that now will make any new attempt more possible.

LESSON No. 4 – BELIEFS ARE A CHOICE

I have met my share of people who can type but believe with all their heart that they can't play the piano. Or people who can keep peas on a fork who don't believe they could ever learn to juggle. It's all very silly when you watch people objectively.

Your beliefs and attitudes play a very significant role in determining how you will approach any new situation. They even determine whether you will make the approach at all.

I am frequently astonished when I stop to analyse my beliefs about myself and things in general. I really do walk around as if those beliefs are the real me; and to the degree that they determine my choices, they are me – or certainly an expression of me. My beliefs are the things I talk about, things I stand up for, fight for and defend. Sometimes I even use them to influence other people. Beliefs are funny things. They're made up in our heads, often independently of direct experience; that's what makes them so fascinating.

Beliefs aren't real. You can't look at one, or touch it; but what we believe dictates how we approach life and especially how we approach learning.

For instance, you will tend to not do things that you believe to be too difficult or too dangerous. You probably won't do things you believe are morally wrong. Every action is weighed up against your beliefs.

My beliefs are an important influence on what I decide I will or won't do. I came to realise that I didn't do well in some learning situations because my beliefs were standing in the way.

SWIMMING AGAINST THE TIDE

Take my attitude towards swimming: it was something to be avoided. Water is wet. Water is often cold. Only in the shower have I found some control over the domain of water.

Training for a triathlon changed all that.

I suppose I could have become a swimmer with my existing set of beliefs, but I would have been a miserable swimmer. The thought of being miserable three times a week while in training would soon have crushed the motivation for the challenge of the triathlon; it would have affected the whole of my physical activity and therefore, ultimately, my health. It was better to work on my beliefs.

I set about examining my beliefs about swimming – and some were really bizarre:

Don't put your head in the water – it's bad for your ears. Your eyes can get infected, bloodshot and itchy. There are things that bite in the water. It is always cold. Drowning, next to burning, is the worst way to die, (except for the part about seeing your life flash before you, which rather fascinated me). People who swim are 'water' people, those who don't, aren't.

There were other beliefs, but that's a taste.

I wrote down my beliefs about the water. At the time they all seemed reasonable to me. As I looked for the source of the belief, I found some surprises.

- *It's bad if you get water in your ears.*

All my childhood, I watched my father swim with his head out of the water and heard my mother warn, "John, don't get water in your ears. "Of course, my father had severe ear damage as a child and water was a danger for him. I, however, didn't have one whit of trouble with my ears and water was no threat. But I became afraid to put my head in the water as a result of this belief.

- *It makes your skin and eyes burn.*

I just knew somehow that chlorine could make you blind. Never mind that I was now swimming in clean ocean water. This belief dates back to the days when there weren't so many backyard pools. Anyone lucky enough to have one found the entire neighbourhood's child population managed to get themselves invited – so the water was chlorinated to the point of instant skin removal.

I also had a few broken arms as a kid – never more than two at a time, of course, and I'd put plastic bags over the cast to go swimming. Sometimes the bags would leak and the chlorine was so strong that it would bleach away the indelible-ink messages friends had written on the cast.

- *There are things that bite in the water.*

I grew up on Long Island Sound of the coast of Connecticut where the water temperature is near to boiling in August and the beaches were closed because of jellyfish, sharks and the like. I used to have nightmares about jellyfish from all the gruesome stories we were told to frighten us into staying away from the beach on a hot day. I saw the movie Jaws when I was 18 in New Jersey – where shark attacks had been a reality. Nevertheless, I carried that belief with me right into the pool at North Sydney, Australia.

- *It's always cold.*

Don't ask me where this comes from. I don't believe it comes from any experience with water – although I do remember coming up blue after falling through the ice while skating on a pond. I think cold was a massive generalisation and the thing I disliked being most. So "I don't like cold" and "I don't like water", simply got linked.

- *Drowning is a terrible way to die.*

I had seen people drown in the movies and it looked horrible. Of course, those people dried off after the shoot and went home for a swim. I have never met anyone who has drowned or at least no-one who has much recollection of the event, anyway!

- *People who swim are water people.*

What does that mean? I believed some people were just meant for the water, others (like myself) were not.

Amazingly, when I look at my beliefs about anything, I find that most of them are linked to someone or some event from my past. I bought it, hook, line and sinker. Usually I can't even remember thinking about whether the belief was logical or how true it was.It's fun to examine what your beliefs are and where they originate; it's even more fun to see all the ways you reinforce the belief once it is set.

I have spent entire nights talking about how awful it is in Florida. It's too hot and humid, there are too many tourist traps, it's far too crowded and no one speaks English. What's interesting is that I have never been to Florida, but it's where my father spent one of the worst weeks of his life.

We tend to dislike what we don't understand.

One night, sit down with a pad and just write down your prevailing beliefs and attitudes. Like:

- People should work hard for their money.
- Only buy what you can afford.
- Politicians are crooks.
- I'm too old to wear jeans.
- If there was more love the world would be a better place.
- Running is bad for your knees.

Then notice what actions that belief either inspires or inhibits and what the result is. What are you most likely to have in your life because of your beliefs and what are you most likely to miss out on?

TO BELIEVE OR NOT TO BELIEVE

Beliefs are not right or wrong – they are simply useful or not so useful. They either enhance your ability to achieve your goals or hinder that ability.

When I decided to venture into the world of triathlons, I had to overcome internal dialogue being shouted over a bullhorn in my brain.

It said:

- "But I can't run."
- "What do you think you're doing?"
- "You have never been a runner."
- "Remember that last time you ran, you nearly killed us."
- "If God had meant you to run, you would have been born an outlaw."

I knew my beliefs about running by simply listening to the monologue running in my head. Needless to say, I had never been a runner. In the few weak attempts I made in my adult life I had discovered, over and over again, that I couldn't complete one trip around the block or one minute of running. Now that was evidence and as a result, I built up a strong set of beliefs about my inability as a runner.

It took me fourteen years of teaching learning strategies and successes in fifty areas or more, most of which were, at first, seemingly impossible, to finally stumble on the fact that I had never learned or been taught how to run. My belief was not only not true, it wasn't useful – it had been keeping me from an honest attempt at learning to run.

Running is something I believed came with the package of being an ordinary human being. Everybody seemed to run as a kid. Some special people even held on to that talent as adults.

I thought, "I ran as a kid, therefore, I should just be able to run now. If I can't, then running has just disappeared from my life."

What I discovered was that the running I did as a kid was not 'running' at all. I honestly don't think I could have run around the block at 10 years old. What I did then was sprint, dodge, and charge. Even as an athletic kid, I was only required to run fast for a short distance.

As an adult I could still run fast for a short distance. With this discovery, my internal chatter and my belief changed to the much more positive "I don't know if I can run."

Today I can run long distances. I have 'learned' how to run one step at a time. Just like I learned everything else. I started by recognising the limiting belief and chose one that was more useful.

OPERATING ON ABSOLUTES

I think the dilemma with beliefs is that we operate as if they are absolutes; they are not. For example, running may be bad for the knees of some people in some situations, especially without some awareness of the process of running. But it's not bad for all knees and it can be good for many hearts.

It's true that if you never run, you won't hurt your knees from running. It doesn't mean you won't hurt your knees in some other way, or end up with a bad back from sitting slouched in a chair watching TV for five hours a night. I have seen more crippled people who have never run than those who have run.

"Running is bad for your knees" is not a bad belief – it just may not be useful in some contexts.

It is vitally important to learn that the set of actions and attitudes associated with being a learner are quite different from those you need to be anything else. So many of the participants in my training sessions try to approach learning with the same set of strategies with which they approach their jobs and, as you'd expect, it is extremely ineffective.

When you are doing your job you are using skills in which you are already competent. There is self-analysis, self-criticism and self expectation – you can easily predict the steps and procedures to reach a goal. But when you jump into a learning situation, you don't know what to expect.

HEALTHY ATTITUDES

In learning, an attitude of "there is no failure, only feedback" is healthy – but you wouldn't want to run your business on that principle. Behaviour is contextual. You need different types of behaviour when you're learning than you need when you're being a doer.

Here are some types of behaviour and attitudes which may have some value in general life, but they won't win any gold stars if you apply them to learning:

- Needing to be right.
- Needing to do things correctly the first time.
- Needing to be better than everyone else.
- Believing some people should succeed while others fail.
- Focusing on what's wrong without equal attention on what's right.

These attitudes and types of behaviour are better suited to winning in a learning environment:

- Giving permission to make mistakes.
- Focusing on feedback during 'programming' time.
- Doing the best you can, so far.
- Recognising that it's not that you can't, it's that you're not able to – yet.
- Focusing on what you can do today better than you could do yesterday.
- Part of learning is figuring it out and the other part is trying it out.

THE ENVIRONMENT MAKES A DIFFERENCE

Beliefs that are useful in one context may be useless in the context of learning. In business, competition is seen as healthy as a means to stimulate the market by producing ever better, more cost-effective products. In the world of sport, competition improves performance. People typically don't break records in training, but they do in the heat of competition. Even young children reel in a fishing line faster if others are present, than they do when they are alone.

Competition in these contexts can be a powerful tool, but in learning it can be destructive. It destroys morale; it pits one student against another when the point of school is not winning, it's learning. Perfectionism is another useless attitude in the learning environment. Many great people are perfectionists and this can be an enormously productive approach. But, when the brain is attempting to learn a skill, it requires excellent effort, not perfect results. How can you do something perfectly if you are only beginning to find out how to do it?

ANYONE FOR TENNIS?

I used to feel impelled to do everything well. If you asked me out for a game of tennis, I would stall for months and practice in secret until I knew I could play with at least a semblance of confidence.

This attitude cost me many adventures and possibly a great deal of fun. When I reached my thirties, I finally realised that this attitude was not very useful. When I decided to develop the Learning to Learn Music program I decided to begin with the piano. To do that I had no choice but to change my attitude and be willing to be a student. I hired a teacher and sat there numb-fingered week after week, my ears burning as red as the sun with embarrassment.

What I learned was that it was all in my own head; my teacher expected me to be a student, I expected me to play well. I learned more in a few months with her than I might have ever learned on my own.

LOOKING LIKE A BEGINNER

I had to overcome my need to be right, to play well now, to look cool. I had to learn that all learning has a phase in which looking stupid is not really looking stupid, it's just looking like a beginner.

LESSON No. 5 – LEARNING FINER LEVELS OF DISTINCTION

"Intelligence is measured by the number of distinctions you can make."

Werner Erhard

So far, we have been listing distinctions about underlying principles that affect your effectiveness as a learner. Now we will look at distinctions that relate to specific strategies for learning.

I often work with students who want to develop their intelligence, not just in a specific skill, but also in learning in general. I too want them to have a high intelligence in reading, retention, recall, note-taking and other study skills. Even though I know they have been doing these things in some form or fashion for most of their lives, they will need finer distinctions if they are to improve their IQ.

For most people 'reading' has only one distinction – it's all just 'reading'. They read everything in the same way, regardless of the content of the text or the purpose of reading in the first place (for example, for pleasure, for study or for recall).

Excellent readers, I have found, are aware of many distinctions; the effect of their posture on reading, their eye movements, concentration, preparation and objectives. They read more effectively as a result.

IMPROVING WITH DISTINCTIONS

Teaching is about adding distinctions to someone's existing skill base. Learning is about recognising that to improve is a matter of learning finer levels of distinction.

When I first picked up the guitar with the idea of transferring skills from my piano experience, I had very few distinctions. I didn't even know whether to begin on an acoustic guitar or an electric guitar. Never before did the notion that "intelligence is measured by the number of distinctions I can make", make so much sense.

I could have been frustrated beyond belief at the size of the transition and the length of time it was going to take.

My first set of distinctions was comprised of: guitar, six strings, left hand on the neck, right hand plays the rhythm. That's it.

Every day's work became about learning a few new distinctions, such as new chord shapes, new positions for my hands, new rhythm patterns, the location of the notes on the neck of the guitar and so on. My teachers were the source of these new distinctions.

Eight months later, I was on stage teaching 40 people to play the guitar in Melbourne. After a year, I had sold my first set of video tapes on Learning To Learn Music. And, 18 months after that first day, I found myself in a television studio in Tulsa, Oklahoma, making a video and playing guitar with Roy Clark, one of the best country guitarists in America.

In developing skills, such as those involved in learning to play a musical instrument, it is important to remember that there is a seemingly endless number of finer levels of distinctions. However, there is a finite, definable set you need to learn to accomplish your own personal goals.

LESSON No. 6 – HOW TO EAT AN ELEPHANT

How many times have you had every good intention to get your work done, but you either didn't know where to begin or you got bogged down by the size of the job?

One key to staying motivated through long or large learning goals is knowing about CHUNKING. This is expressed in the old joke: "How do you eat an elephant?"

"One bite at a time."

It is not quite that simple though – there are a few catches. What if the bites you take are itsy-bitsy-teeny-weeny bites? Well, then you take a bite, and another, and another, and it looks like the way you're going you'll never get that elephant eaten. Each small bite doesn't seem to be getting you any closer to your goal and you're probably going to get bored eating elephant at this pace. The bites, or chunks, are just too small.

But what if the bites are huge, big mouthfuls? You chew, and chew, and chew, and still have trouble swallowing. You'll be working hard, but each bite will require so much energy you'll probably end up feeling you'll never eat the elephant. The chunks are just too big.

BITE-SIZED CHUNKS

Often, when we jump into a learning situation, the prime concern is the size of the task. It is too big. Chunking is breaking the task down into bite-sized pieces.

Let's say you have a 200-page textbook to read for your night class and you have, of course, decided that every one of those pages is important to read. I know from experience that most adults, like most students, will either wait until the last day and read them all, or they will read them all right now to get the work out of the way. Then there are those who won't read them at all – and pray. All of these strategies, as you will discover, are obstacles to effective study.

When I sit down to study, the FIRST thing I do is look at the size of the task and break it down so it's manageable. If my objective is to read the book by the end of a week, then the task looks a lot different if I know I have about 28 pages to read and comprehend each day. Twenty-eight pages is no big deal and if I commit myself to do whatever it takes to keep up the job, it will get done. And, at the end of every day, I feel good because I am one step closer. This 'feel-good' is usually the motivation I need for the next session.

This works for everything I study or learn to do. When I started running, (which I could not do even in my imagination), the thought of running five kilometres was overwhelming – I never started. Finally, at 35 years old I figured I'd give myself 16 weeks to learn to run five kilometres. The first week I ran three times, and I started by running for one minute and walking for four minutes. I did nine sets of this, a total of 45 minutes. In the third week I changed. I ran for two minutes and walked for three. During the fifth week I had a breakthrough-I ran for six minutes without stopping! From there, improving performance is just a matter of adding small increments to each run. I was running my five kilometres long before 16 weeks had passed.

Now, how many 16-week blocks had already passed in my life? Heaps! And in all of the previous ones, I had never learned to run. The CHUNK SIZE was just too BIG.

BRAIN ENERGY

There are other advantages to chunking your tasks. First, you accelerate the learning process. If you use your brain energy to master one small piece at a time, you won't waste energy trying to focus on too much too soon.

You feel that you're actually getting somewhere. Every day, you will see something you can now do that you couldn't do yesterday. That feeling of success makes time pass quickly. The process speeds up so fast that you can't remember when you couldn't do the task.

When you begin to apply the strategies that follow, please remember that the underlying principle is chunking.

Don't become an 80-year-old who never started simply because it all looked too big. Anyone who excels at anything has done it one step at a time. The only difference between them and you is that they did it, while most of us simply sit at home and dream about it.

The effort you put in will show up when you are compared to others. Let's say you're studying the guitar; the average student does an hour of practice each week. If you do an hour of practice every day, at the end of one week you will have seven weeks of experience compared to the average student. If you do two hours of practice every day, at the end of a week you'll have an equivalent of three-and-a-half months' experience. All in just one week. It is worth it to play around with your time frames. When I saw time this way, I found all kinds of motivation to pick up my guitar, or my French books, or run that extra five kilometres.

SETTING TIME FRAMES

With this understanding, the world of learning changed for me. I found I needed to work in a realistic time frame. So many of my goals are just too big to think about on a daily basis. If I want to become a great guitarist, then I can't expect to move from where I am today to the state of great guitarist, in just one practice session.

I use all kinds of time frames when I set a goal for myself. I set up measuring sticks for various lengths of time into the future. The goal of being a great guitarist is not a useful one for me to carry into today's practice session. But the goal of being just a hair faster, or a bit smoother, really is useful. It's achievable, and I know I won't ever be a great guitarist if I don't focus on the short-term goal of picking up my speed.

Stephanie Burns

A HEAVY LOAD ON THE EARS

When I begin something new, I find it very hard to stay with it because I am usually so lousy at it. Hearing yourself play an instrument for the first few months, maybe even years, can put a heavy load on your ears. I still have trouble listening to myself play without comparing myself to every other guitarist I hear on the radio. I make commitments to stick with things, no matter what, for a certain time.

I say, "I will play for 30 minutes a day, (no matter what I think about my playing), every day for 90 days." I then set up a calendar and tick off the days after I have done my 30 minutes. This takes the pressure off me and I don't worry about what I sound like. It doesn't matter. The only thing that matters is that I put in the time. In 90 days there will inevitably have been some improvement and that is a better time than today to evaluate my progress. What I usually find is that there is so much improvement that I am motivated to go another 90 days.

GETTING HOOKED

You can't say today what you will do every day, forever. But you can evaluate fairly well your ability to do something consistently for a short time – let's say a month – and at the end of the month you can choose again. If you're noticing your successes my bet is you'll choose it again for another short stint. Before you know it, a few years have passed and you're hooked.

I do this at the gym. If I thought I'd have to work out for the rest of my life, I'd quit today. But I use the gym for very specific goals linked to my triathlon training. It may be to add bulk. It may be to improve my strength and endurance. For this, the gym is great. But I never commit to a gym program for more than three months. I can't see much gain any further ahead than that. I break that down and know that if I go to the gym, somehow, (no matter what), three times a week for 13 weeks, a mere 39 sessions, I will achieve a significant change in my performance.

So without thinking about it, just ticking off times on my calendar, I get my butt to the gym three times a week. When I am there I do what I have to do. When I'm done, I pack up, walk out, no big deal. When I get home I put a tick on my calendar – another one done. It's easy to put 39 ticks on my calendar. Some days, I go to the gym just so I can have another tick. In three months the changes are usually so significant, that the next time the gym is needed it's an easier choice to make.

It's important to understand that most goals are really lifelong pursuits. That's what is so surprising; we can't see ourselves doing something about our goals every day of our life – it's too long. We spend our lives doing things like going to work or doing laundry and never put in a bit of time to do things that would improve the quality of our lives, the quality of our thinking.

TWO-TIMING

Sixteen hours of time awake is A LOT. But only if you stay aware of the minutes – the time that there is. It's easy to fritter away days, weeks, even months without awareness. How do I get so much done in a day? I have two different types of time running in the day.

I have FIXED TIME hours in each day allocated to certain activities. In those hours I have a plan. Anything that I feel HAS to get done, like writing or training, gets planned for those hours, usually the night before. If I don't do these things by bedtime the next day I'll feel a fair bit of stress. I've chosen my best personal hours for these. They are the first few hours in the day after waking up and the late afternoon or early evening hours before dinner – perhaps you are best at different times.

And then I have FLEXIBLE TIME. I use my lousiest personal time for that, which for me is the afternoon. I am so lethargic then that I'm just as likely to choose a nap as anything else. I use this kind of time for the miscellany of other activities that can otherwise destroy a day. I don't know usually what I will do during that time – I leave it to the moment. It allows me to do whatever I feel like doing. Sometimes that's lunch with a friend, sometimes a sleep, sometimes I read, sometimes I do the shopping, sometimes I iron… whatever.

In this way I have guaranteed myself a fixed set of time that is planned ahead and a set of flexible hours for the 'whatevers'. There is never a day when I don't accomplish what I planned to do.

People who work in a full-time job already have a large block of fixed time in their day. But that still leaves eight hours to play with. Many will have other fixed blocks of time for family needs and other commitments, but that still leaves time for your own goals.

Take any activity you have wanted to pursue and fix some time for it in your day. Don't let anything get in the way of keeping that time for yourself. It might mean getting up half an hour earlier, or going to bed half an hour later. But begin.

LESSON No. 7 – FEELINGS ARE NOT FACTS!

We confront many experiences in our first years. The brain works to categorise what it is experiencing to create meaning. It develops handy labels for our feelings. We have an experience, get a feeling in our body and attach a label to that feeling. When we have that experience again, we call up the same label. When beginning something new we often experience a tightening in our stomach, a weak feeling in our limbs and the label we attach to those feelings is often: 'discomfort', 'anxiety', 'not right', 'foolish' or 'silly'.

We then do whatever it takes to alleviate or change those feelings – usually by stopping what we're doing or going back to something more familiar.

FROM QUEASY TO EASY

I encounter this "going back to something more familiar" with a lot of competent, but none the less, "middle of the road" musicians. When given some new challenge, they'll give it a good effort, then start playing songs and ditties they've been playing all their life. It felt better to play what was familiar than to cope with the feelings they experienced when learning something new.

What they fail to realise, however, is that they felt those same queasy feelings learning what they now do so well. If they don't take the new skills through that stage, it will always feel awkward. I've even heard excellent musicians proclaim loudly that they can do 'x' but not 'y.' But it's only that they learned 'x' first and have become comfortable with it.

DEALING WITH A SHAKY BODY

What we already know can stand in the way of learning something new. In most new experiences your body will feel a bit shaky and it will do so until the new behaviour or skill becomes natural or familiar.

One game in learning is to find a useful label for those feelings – to recognise that those are the feelings associated with learning and that they will change as soon as your nervous system gets the hang of what you're trying to do.

Recognising that you will go through a period of feeling uncomfortable can greatly ease the learning of new skills, especially if you are learning something physical.

In some cases, it can even make the difference that stops you from quitting the learning process altogether.

It does heaps of good to recall some of your past learning experiences, describe the feelings you had, and remind yourself that these feelings are a natural part of learning and have accompanied every new endeavour. This way, when you venture into the new experience, you can better understand the feelings you will have and will be less likely to avoid the new task. You will give yourself a comfortable feeling about being uncomfortable.

THE GREAT MOTORCYCLE ADVENTURE

I was 28 years old when I decided to learn to ride a motorcycle. Of course, not only did I need to contend with being right out of my comfort zone, I also had to deal with my need to do things well before anyone could watch.

I bought a beautiful, black-and-chrome Kawasaki 550, bluffing my way through and by-passing a test ride. The salesman couldn't figure out why I didn't want to ride the bike away, but instead had it delivered to my home on the back of a trailer.

For the first week I just sat on it. Every time I did that I became more frightened. Eventually I started it up, let it idle, decided that was enough for my nervous system to handle in one day and turned it off.

A week or so later, when I'd recovered and had read everything I could find on how to ride a motorcycle, I eased it along in first gear down the driveway. Of course, I was too afraid to turn the bike around, so after reaching the end of the driveway I'd walk it back and do it again. It took a week, but eventually I felt just less than nauseous riding the bike around the block.

I felt so uncomfortable that I noticed I'd find any excuse to take the car. I'd just had my nails done. It might rain. I might meet a friend and want to have them come along. Of course, this meant the bike sat idle.

RIDING THROUGH THE COMFORT ZONE

I finally realised that I would never learn to ride confidently if I didn't do it often enough. So being me, I sold my car. I then only had the bike. The strategy of preferring to stay home with any excuse, rather than ride, eventually wore thin and my adventures began. First, I had a contract to teach in the city coming up and in Los Angeles there's no alternative to your own personal transport to get anywhere. So I had no choice but to get on the bike. I put my work clothes, an iron, and a hair dryer in my bike bag and eased my way into town.

Needless to say, I made it. This was the day I brought the bike just into reach of my comfort zone. Everyday after, inspired by this new feeling of riding, I found new places to go and new things to learn.

In less than two weeks my transition was complete. I certainly was as comfortable on the bike as I had been in my car. I wondered why I'd let it take me months of discomfort to simply put in the two weeks of riding I needed. For 18 months I stayed with the bike as my sole transport, and one thing I'll say is that you will go places on a bike that wouldn't interest you in the least in a car.

I'm not an advocate of a bike for everyone, but I can say that learning about riding a motorcycle was really about learning a lot of new things about life, and an adventure for me. You might also discover that taking on the challenge to learn one new thing, will most often times net you with a hundred new things you didn't know about before.

REMEMBER THE FEELINGS OF LEARNING

Adults have forgotten what it feels like in their body when their body is stimulated in new ways. That it feels like 'this'. The 'this' can be loud internal dialogue, or rumblings in the stomach, or clenched teeth and have labels attached to them. Those feelings when labelled by most adults are called anxiety, stress, discomfort. The label isn't the fact. It's just a feeling, an emotional or physical signal.

If a feeling is labelled as discomfort the natural human tendency is to do something to change the feeling. In a learning situation this action is to return to a past habitual behaviour that is familiar. Yet we all know that repeating a past behaviour has nothing to do with learning a new one. It's just reinforcing a behaviour such that it is even stronger the next time.

Adult learners can be frustrated to no end, because they have a belief that they should be able to perform some new skill at the highest level of competence as soon as they are introduced to it. If I had my way, I would see that every adult had one experience of taking a new skill, or new choice, or new way of thinking through their comfort zone to the point at which they experienced comfort.

LESSON No. 8 – IF YOU CAN'T REMEMBER IT, YOU DIDN'T LEARN IT

Think about some of the things you need to remember in typical learning and work situations.

Names and dates

Historical facts

Lines from books and poems

Numbers and formulae

Lists of things

Correct spelling

New vocabulary

Each one of these types of information and many others use the same strategy.

More important than all other skills, you will need the ones of remembering what you have learned.

Think about all the effort you put into learning, be it facts for your next presentation, numbers for the board meeting, or a new technique on the computer. That effort is worthless if you are not able to access that information or skill when it is needed.

I have found student after student defeated simply because they cannot remember what they learn. This experience makes it easy to come to the conclusion that you have a bad memory. But, without actual brain damage, it is almost impossible to have a bad memory. You can, however, interpret mistakes and forgotten information as evidence of a poor memory. That evidence you use to create a belief about your memory can be strong enough to plague you all your life. Without doubt, you can become very good at forgetting.

It's also important to note that each of us works with our brain a bit differently. You may need to experiment to find your own strengths.

MAKING PICTURES IN YOUR HEAD

The most powerful sense for us is sight. We are easily stimulated by visual input and most of what you know is based on strong visual memory. Some people are just great at making pictures in their heads, others need to use sounds, or music, or language to reinforce their memories; while others need to use body motion to build strong memories. I'll give you some examples of all of these.

Forgetting information has nothing to do with your memory. It has to do with failing to make information memorable in the first place and that provides you with a good strategy for forgetting.

Let's look at a few examples:

1) *You've read the chapter you were assigned at your night class and immediately upon finishing, you turn to the practice questions at the end of the chapter. The information just doesn't seem to be in you head and you have to turn back to the text.*

2) *A trainer leading a seminar tells you there are three essential reasons why justice works. At the end of her lecture you pick up a pen to write them down – but you can only remember the first one.*

3) *You've been asked to remember to get a paper signed by your spouse. You don't remember it until the lady at the dry cleaners asks if this paper belongs to you.*

THERE ARE TWO PARTS TO REMEMBERING!

These examples show the problem when the first of these two parts is missing – you haven't done something to make information memorable.

DROPPING YOUR LUNCH

You process such a small amount of the information that comes in through your senses that I don't even know how to write a number that small. One primary function of your brain is to delete information. It is also designed to be attracted to, or stimulated by, information that is different from the norm. If you want facts, data, faces, events or places to be remembered, you need to actively make them memorable by making them different. If you don't make them memorable, you will simply remember whatever attracts your brain's attention most.

For example, you may forget your lessons at the end of a school day, but you will remember the student who dropped his lunch in his lap. I don't want to know how you forget the lessons – I want to know how you remembered the useless event of the dropped lunch.

If the information in the classes you attend is always presented in the same way, your brain goes into idle. It will sit like that until something attracts its attention. The teacher does a weird thing, or someone in class twists the information around so that it's funny, or you doodle it in your notebook. Memory doesn't just happen, you have to do something.

BRAIN ALERT!

No doubt, when the plate of lunch dropped it shocked you – your brain was alerted. You may have laughed if a piece of mashed potato ended up in someone's face. All of these things highlight the event and make it easy to remember.

If a presenter took the date 1907, wrote it on the board and said you have to remember this number, most of you would forget it by the next day. But if she spray painted it on the front of her desk, and she had never done this before, you'd remember it 20 years later.

A PIECE OF PIE

It's not the information – it's what you do to the information that counts.

Suppose I wanted you to remember how to spell the word 'piece'. Many of you could simply build a very strong picture of the word. You could imagine the word written like this:

P IE CE

Here, you are exaggerating the part of the word you typically find confusing.

Or you might make an internal picture like this:

PIE CE

Here, you are using a word you are already familiar with, 'pie', as the memory trigger. This makes the image unique and much easier to recall later. If you look at the word printed that way and then close your eyes and make a mental picture, in a moment you will have the image installed solidly enough for there to be no confusion in spelling the word. You will simply recall that picture and spell. If you focused on the internal image, you would even be able to comfortably spell it backwards. You're reading it off your internal blackboard.

YOUR SENSE SYSTEMS

Some people, however, need to use their auditory (sound) or kinaesthetic (physical) senses. Some of you will have better recall if you sound out the word, emphasizing with a different tone of voice the two letters 'I' and 'E'. Others who are good with their auditory memory find that linking the information to a song helps, replacing the song's lyrics with the facts they need to remember. Rap music is now being used by lots of teens to remember their school work. When you spell the word, you hear these two letters accented or marked uniquely.

Some of you will need to get your bodies involved. You may find it helps to spell the word out in the air using your arm, again making the I and E bigger than the rest of the letters. This whole-body experience is excellent for reinforcing memories you are installing. Many students go down to the beach and write words in the sand, or use stones to spell them out. For these people, getting the memory into the system by acting it out is the key.

So, in all the following examples of making information memorable, it is important to know that you have all of these systems. Some are stronger than others in all of us. Once you have found the way that produces a success for you every time, you'll have your own keys for successful memory.

TRIGGER HAPPY

Here is the second important part to remembering: Once the information has been made memorable it has to be linked to a trigger so it can be recalled at the appropriate time.

There is no sense in making information memorable if you can't recall it when you need it. How many of you have had the experience of struggling to find an answer you knew was in your head while taking an exam and then had the frustration of remembering it when you left the classroom?

When the second part of a good memory strategy fails, here's what happens:

1) *Mary goes through her morning routine and heads off to work. She arrives at her office, and as she hears the click of the lock on the filing cabinet, she seizes up and says, "Aghhh, I forgot the files!" She then says, "I worked on them all night and then I forgot them."*

2) *John swallows his last sip of coffee, grabs his bag and heads out the door. Just as he's about to grab the handle of his car door, he realises he's locked his keys in the house. He spends the next hour getting a locksmith to let him back in, and during that time he continually tells himself how stupid he is that he couldn't even remember his keys. It's the third time he's locked his keys in the house this month.*

3) *Shaun shows up at night school and immediately on seeing Sarah he remembers that he has forgotten the book he'd promised her. He's had to apologise every day this week.*

Is it true that these people have forgotten?

NO! The information (like remembering the book), has been stored. However, it was remembered at a not very useful time. What use is it to remember your keys after you've locked the house? It is not that these people have bad memories – they have just demonstrated a great memory. The memory, however, is linked to the wrong trigger.

There are three components that make for strong memories and memory links.

The first component of strong memories involves your five senses. Sight, sound, taste, touch and smell. Things that are memorable often have a strong relationship to the five senses. As I said earlier, we process and therefore remember very little that comes in through our senses. But our memories have a strong link to sensory information.

If you were walking down a street in New York with 50 million people coming at you, would you expect to remember all of them? Of course not. But a lot of people will tell me they have a bad memory because they can't. Without some action to make people memorable, they will slip through the net of your brain. Who would you remember at the end of the day?

You would remember anyone who stood out as being different or unique. Their uniqueness is what stimulated your brain to notice them in the first place, and then their uniqueness contributed to them becoming memorable. For example, someone wearing a banana suit, or an old lady wearing a diaper. Someone with a strange hairstyle, someone carrying a boa constrictor, someone who flashed you or even someone who mugged you. In all these cases, the person would be different enough to catch your brain's attention. If you go one step further and imagine yourself telling your spouse tonight and him or her laughing hysterically, you will have a strong enough trigger to see that the event is recalled when you see your spouse.

USE YOUR IMAGINATION

If you want information to be remembered, MAKE IT UNIQUE. Single bits of data are easy. Many times each day, I'm given some bit of information to remember and running around finding a scrap of paper wastes too much time. If I get a call saying tomorrow I'm on Qantas flight 27 at 8am, I need to make that memorable. So I make the information as strange and weird as I can.

In my imagination I might see an Qantas jet. This one's different because it's parked with its nose in the terminal. Written on the side in neon letters is the number 27. And blasting out of a speaker in the nose is a squeaking voice saying "We leave at 8am."

Another way I might do this is to look at my wristwatch and imagine the hands are at 8am; lifting off out of the face is a tiny Qantas jet and when I look really close, the wings are oddly shaped – one looks like a 2, the other like a 7. I catch the jet in my fingers, say "So long, flight 27" and squash it.

One more way might be to imagine that I've lay down on the runway. I hear a tremendous roar, and as I lift my head up, I see a Qantas jet bearing down on me. As it passes over me I see the number 27 in neon lights on the belly. When it's gone by, I'm left looking at the sky and there's a huge clock hanging in thin air. What's the time? That's right, it's 8am.

FIVE BILLION BRAINS

There is no one right way to make information memorable. When I have my students do an exercise like this in my seminar, it is fascinating that no two brains have come up with the same story, image or sound. There are many billions of people on the planet, and that many different ways of doing this. But you must do something to make the information different. In these cases, I used my senses to exaggerate the data.

Do you still remember the date the teacher painted on the front of the desk?

EMOTIONS and REPETITION are the other components of strong memories and memory links. Emotions create strong links to the past. Most of us can conjure up vivid memories when we think of EMBARRASSING situations, or FEARFUL situations, or even JOYFUL situations. If you can exaggerate the emotions involved with your experiences, they will stick much better. Instead of fun, make it extreme fun, instead of excited, make it very excited.

Repetition is the only memory strategy I recall using in school. Remember reading chapters over and over again in the hope that they would stick? Repetition, though, does have a role to play – if you want information to stick firmly in your long-term memory then you will need to do a bit of repetition.

The key to all of these strategies is the use of UNIQUENESS.

Regardless of whether you choose to use EMOTIONAL or SENSORY based stimulants, or plain old REPETITION, the key is to make it unique – make it different. If I want to remember a kelpie is a sheepdog then I need to make that kelpie unique and link it to a unique sheep. If I think of a regular old kelpie as a plain old dog, how will it be strong enough to remember? I will want to make the kelpie really big and have it eat a sheep. Or really little kelpies sitting on the nose of huge green sheep. Whatever, but it must capture my imagination.

Once I have established the information as memorable I will need to do a bit of repetition over the course of the day, over the course of the week. This repetition, fortunately, can be done in the privacy of your own mind whenever you have a spare minute in your head; for instance, when you're walking between classes or during a particularly boring part of class.

JOINING THE LINKS

Once information is made memorable, how are you going to recall that information when you need it? You don't want the trigger for work you've done at home to be something in your office. If that happens you will perpetually remember the report too late to see that it gets from home to work.

To remember to bring your report to work, you might imagine yourself eating your usual breakfast. Maybe it's eggs. Imagine that you look down to take a bite out of your eggs and someone's standing in them – your boss – and he's yelling, "Don't forget the report."

At breakfast tomorrow, (if you rehearse this a few times), you will remember the report. That's a much better trigger than waiting till you reach your office.

It is important to recognise that this is how you remember what you do anyway. Information has been made memorable and it has been linked to a trigger. We are forcing the issue – making it memorable and making a link.

RIGHT PLACE, RIGHT TIME

Why do you forget the answers when you are taking the test in the classroom, but remember them later on? The two most common reasons are because the information was never made very memorable in the first place, and because the information wasn't linked to that classroom during that situation.

When I am studying, I imagine myself in the place where I am going to need the information I am taking in. As you make facts memorable for a test, decide where you want the link. Perhaps it will be to your desk or to the test paper; imagine the questions being written, again in some unique way and see yourself having the memory of the answer.

Many times when we study we say to ourselves "I'll never remember this," and then we wonder why we don't. Our focus is on forgetting, so we link forgetting instead of remembering to the situation.

Your internal dialogue, your self-talk, is also an important part of your memory strategy.

LESSON No. 9 – THE ART OF TAKING NOTES

There is only one reason for taking notes – that is, as a mechanism for remembering or reviewing what you have learnt. If your notes aren't serving this one purpose my advice is: DON'T BOTHER.

There are two types of things that you learn. You learn new skills, meaning things that you DO with your body – actions. You also learn information, data, facts, and ideas – things that you want to KNOW. Note taking is primarily useful for this second type of learning. Once your nervous system has mastered a skill, it needs physical rehearsal to maintain or improve it. In the same way, new information also needs rehearsal to fix it as a permanent part of your thinking.

When you first learn new information, it sits very precariously in your mind unless it has been given to you in a highly memorable way. You need some means to transfer your new facts and information from short-term memory to long-term memory, which is where notes come into play. Notes are the means for stimulating or refreshing your brain. If you apply the rules of making it memorable, you'll spend less time studying.

THE PARTY BORE

Think for a minute. How many pages of notes have you taken and never looked at again? Most adult students never look at their notes after writing them. So what good are they?

We don't look at our notes for the same reason that most information gets lost when we write it down. It's boring. It's all the same.

When you take notes using a ballpoint pen on white paper, writing the same size, the same shape and within the same margins, you are setting up some very non-memorable notes. When you look at your notes and they all look the same, your brain automatically drops out of gear.

Your notes should fulfil two roles:

- they should excite you to look at them, and
- they should make the information memorable.

If you studied the section on MAKING INFORMATION MEMORABLE, you already know how to do this. Your notes need to be different or unique. What can you do to make notes different? Well, lots of things.

- Use coloured markers. Your brain loves colour – it is attracted immediately to notes using bright colours.

- Write in different sizes. When your eye is scanning your notes it will look more like a picture than like words, and your brain really has fun with stimulating images.

- Draw pictures and symbols. My notes are full of arrows, ticks, dashes, numbers, and drawings. The old saying about a picture being worth a thousand words is somewhat true. If you can capture the data in an image, it'll stick.

- Experiment with something other than linear writing. Which law says you have to write from the top of the page to the bottom? For one week see what happens when you write from the bottom to the top.

A NOTE FOR STUDENTS WHO MAY NOT BE ALLOWED TO USE COLOURED MARKERS

This happens to a lot of students who want to try something new. They are told it isn't allowed. I know of students whose coloured pens were confiscated, or who were ridiculed by a teacher, or by other students, because their notes looked different.

If this happens to you, I can make two recommendations that are within the realms of possibility.

The riskier of the two is to ask the teacher for a meeting, where you can ask for permission to try something new for a month and that if you do it responsibly and your grades improve, that you be allowed to continue. If you write on the desk, or there's no change in your work, you'll go back to the way the teacher wants you to do it.

There's no harm in asking. All anyone can say is no.

If that doesn't seem possible for you, I suggest you rewrite your notes as part of your study time. Reviewing notes is a sufficiently important part of the transfer from short-term to long-term memory to warrant the time.

LESSON No. 10 – THE IMPORTANCE OF WORDS

Why all this noise about vocabulary? Students are up to their ears in vocabulary. You may remember those 20 word lists you had to learn at school. I really wish I could give you the good news that vocabulary doesn't matter, but it does. It's very important and most successes in learning depend on it.

Unfortunately, IF YOU DON'T USE IT YOU LOSE IT.

Most of the words were really important. Unfortunately, most of us didn't use those words then, don't use those words now, the teacher didn't use them, and most of the words you put your time into learning didn't match up with what you read during those years, either.

HAVE YOU GOT A WORD DEFICIENCY?

Many adults suffer the penalty of a poorly established vocabulary.

Many poor results in school eventually boil down to vocabulary deficiencies. Did you know that two out of four answers in most multiple choice tests can be eliminated if you understand the meaning of the words in the question and the answer? We fail a lot of tests and courses because we don't understand the language.

Successful people have better vocabularies. This is how they have a better-than-average understanding of what they read and what they hear, and it's why they're so good at selling their ideas to others.

Often, when you find yourself failing in a learning situation, it's because you are confused by the concepts, not because you're not trying or are not smart enough to learn. If you don't understand the words used in the books you read, you can't fully understand the content and the problem compounds itself with every lesson.

When you don't know the meaning of a word you're reading, your brain ignores it. Do you ever wonder why you have poor comprehension after reading, no matter how many times you've read it over? One of the reasons is that your brain doesn't get an accurate picture of the data.

THE ESSENTIAL VOCABULARY

I am not an advocate of going to the dictionary and looking up lots of words to learn. You won't use them, so they won't stick. You tried this in school – it didn't work then and it won't work now.

The absolutely essential vocabulary is made up of the words in the books you read or that your teacher uses to describe a concept or idea. You will save yourself an almost unimaginable amount of work if you simply understand the language better. A trainer's lecture or the concepts in books will make sense the first time you hear or read them, and you will save study time by not having to go over and over material you're unlikely to understand in a hundred years.

THE PLAN OF ATTACK

The words you need to know are in the books and magazines you will find in your home or office. It would be good to get one and open it to the beginning. Using a light pencil scan through the text and put a tick by any words that are unfamiliar.

DON'T MAKE THE TASK TOO HARD.

You don't have to read the text to find these words. If you do a quick scan they'll stand out. Just tell your brain look for any word pattern for which it has no definition.

KEEP IT SIMPLE – ROME WASN'T BUILT IN A DAY.

When you have ten words, pull out a notebook and write them down. Grab a dictionary or ask someone for the word's definition. Then go and memorise these words. Use the MAKE IT MEMORABLE section in this book for a good, quick strategy to get the words from the page to your brain.

WHAT TO DO WHEN YOU'VE GOT THEM

It's important now that you read the text knowing the definition. It will teach you how to use the word properly. You might even put the words into a few sentences when you talk with others.

REMEMBER THOUGH, YOU HAVE A COMFORT ZONE.

New language is like any new skill. It takes a few repetitions before the words will come out naturally. As you've learned, if you don't use the words they'll disappear and your work will be wasted. And if you don't use them, they will never be comfortable to use.

WHY THESE WORDS?

Because these are the words, specifically, that will make a difference.

This little exercise of ten words (perhaps every second day) is going to save you heaps of time, improve your memory through practice, and increase your understanding of the material that matters to you most.

IF YOU ARE IN SCHOOL OR HAVE CHILDREN IN SCHOOL:

Many students fail because they do not understand the words they read and hear. They can derive quick and lasting benefit from going through the first few chapters in every textbook and getting a handle on the vocabulary. When a student gets confused it is often because of vocabulary, and the problem compounds itself into unmanageable proportions as the weeks go on. It's best to attempt to stay a couple of chapters ahead, just to be on top of the essential vocabulary.

LESSON No. 11 – BEING GREAT IS A CHOICE

It is said that great men and women are not born but made. Maybe that is so. People who achieve greatness seem to continuously be learning. They understand that learning is a process; that failures provide feedback for the next attempt. They don't quit easily and they are committed to doing whatever it takes to succeed. These people place a high value on time. They don't take the world too seriously and they have the ability to laugh at themselves.

But should everyone aspire to greatness? I don't believe so. But I do believe it is important that everyone should be given the opportunity to know that being excellent at something is possible. I believe you should know the truth that to be 'great' is a choice – indeed, I see it as a universal right.

You need to understand that the strategies needed to bring dreams to fruition are also your right and that you should have access to those strategies. You have the right to be treated like a human being, with all that being human entails – the recognition and development of your tremendous learning potential.

I believe people should be encouraged to be the best they can be, be they solicitor, clerk, truck driver or teacher. When you are treated like an idiot, you learn to behave like an idiot, but not because you are an idiot.

THE PATH TO GREATNESS

Great is the person who makes a difference, who uses the resources of their brain to benefit not just themselves but everyone they meet. Great is the teacher who teaches all day and studies at night. Great is the coach who shows you a new way. Great is the nurse who smiles and instils hope for tomorrow. Great is about knowing how to do small things that make significant differences.

The world has a crying need for great minds, great thinkers and great technicians. The world's complexity means that our great managers and maintainers are too thinly spread; the few who stumble on the path to greatness are not enough. The technology exists today to offer the opportunity for greatness to everyone.

So What?

"The difference between intelligence and education is this: intelligence will make you a good living."

Charles F. Kettering

SO WHAT IF YOU DIDN'T DO WELL AT SCHOOL?

I believe we are at a turning point in history – but then again many people in every generation have said that. Schools were designed with the best of intentions and were relatively successful in meeting the needs of a world very different from ours.

Schools succeeded for the time when large numbers of people had to acquire basic skills and discipline to enter the workforce. Schools were designed to teach a student the skills of acquiring facts and data and to then follow instructions as to what to do with those facts and data. The world of a hundred years ago needed men – and some women – who could read and write, do simple maths, follow directions, be on time and sit at a desk for a long day.

Schools did a good job of preparing people to fit into this kind of world. Until the early 1950s, I don't believe people had too many qualms about how school was doing its job. It was based on the needs of the future workforce and was successful at meeting those demands. Schools mirrored how the majority of the people in the workforce functioned and prepared them to enter it.

It is critical to note that before the mid-1940s the world was relatively quiet. Compared to a child's home life, school was likely perceived as exciting – it was a place to be stimulated, and learning is about stimulating the nervous system to grow and adapt. For a child back then, going to school to read books, sit at a desk, take notes and hear a teacher's lecture was fun.

But everything has changed. Specifically, the world outside school has become enormously stimulating, crammed with marvels like television, video games, computers, fast cars, complex music, extreme sports and high-speed travel. We take highly stimulated children and confine them in restrictive classrooms with blue ink on white paper, white chalk on black boards, old films and boring books – and, just as you'd expect, they go crazy. If learning is to happen, there must be difference – unique situations, events that stimulate the brain and grab your attention. Asking a child today to sit still and listen to slow-paced lectures, and to read uninteresting texts, creates problems we are only just beginning to come to terms with.

Since Elvis Presley hit the scene in the 1950's, young people have experienced an ever-increasing level of stimulus. The world outside was able to offer so much more excitement and variety that the traditional school environment appeared to have less and less to offer. It is any wonder children don't want to be there.

Remember too, that school was not designed to provide the world with great thinkers, although it did produce some. The few leaders the world needed learned their skills primarily from life experience – not from school experience. The world needed more workers than thinkers, more skilled hands than managers, more followers than leaders, more who could simply read a report than those who could write a report. School has done what it was designed to do.

Today, there's a fundamental conflict. Success in school requires quite different skills from those needed to succeed even in the most basic of jobs. That's why we read about so many success stories of those who didn't survive their school experience. But that is not really surprising; it has always been this way.

School performance does not predict life success.

Today, we have the knowledge to understand how traditional approaches to education undermine the natural learning systems of the human brain and body. We are taught to use alien and often useless ways of thinking, being, and doing. It's important to recognise that they weren't alien back then – but now they are.

SLOW CHANGE

Schools are large systems. School policy and management today is usually decided by people typically in their late 50's or 60's – men and women who were in the 5th grade in the 1940s and 50s. They were the last generation for whom the current school structure was appropriate and they are still attempting to recreate the school structures that worked so well for them. Curriculum and teaching styles matched their view of the world in which the majority of students were going to live. It's why we so often hear the catch cry "back to basics" in the often times heated debate about education. I believe that "back to basics" is a death rattle for the education of today's children.

I see a lot of evidence that schools and teachers are trying very hard to move with the times. But why aren't they changing faster? I believe it is because although we know that school does not match up with the world our children will inherit, there is little agreement on what the objectives of education should be. We used to be able to look forward twenty years and have a fairly good idea of what the future would hold. Things didn't move so quickly as to preclude good predictions. Schools prepared young people accordingly. But who, in 1940, could have predicted the world we live in today? Why is the education system not responding in ways the public thinks it should? They don't have a clue what the world will look like five years from now, let alone twenty.

IT'S NOT THAT WE CHANGE, IT'S THAT THE ENVIRONMENT CHANGES

As classroom styles change, so does our performance. It is said that we learn more from birth to four years than we do cumulatively in the rest of our lives. I do not know if this is indeed an accurate representation, but it certainly has a ring to it. Look at the environment for learning and the permission given for being a learner to very young children – walk into a day care centre and you will see the best approach to whole-brain learning in full swing. Colour, sound, music, movement, storytelling, use of active imagination, hands-on experimentation and plenty more. Our brain doesn't lose its ability to learn as we did when we were young. It is still capable of doing all that – and better – as we get older. The brain seems to change in stages and with each stage a new quality of thinking becomes available. Our ability to learn, by rights, should be jumping ahead in leaps and bounds as our brains develop.

It isn't the student's ability to learn that changes so dramatically – it's the approach to teaching that changes. A child's abilities in school change, often for the worse, at the same time that schools change their approach. Few seem to be making the link.

WHO ARE YOU CALLING STUPID?!

It puzzles me that with the new knowledge we have about learning, we still persist in labelling a child with poor school performance as "stupid" – even though we know the child is likely to generalise that label to every activity. Yet one day that child may read about great people who were labelled stupid – and then we'll look stupid.

We have all the data, but the territory is being mapped incorrectly. It's not that students aren't learning – they are. They cannot NOT learn. However, is what they learn essential for the future they will inherit? That's a better question. If the system were really the failure we read so much about in the newspapers, how did you ever get where you are?

IS THE SYSTEM FAILING?

The education system is charged with the duty of preparing young minds and bodies for the future. Is it failing? In many situations the answer is yes. It is ignoring thirty years of research and evidence about learning. In desperation, it has at times become susceptible to pop psychology and that has done more harm than good. Some students don't succeed – some don't even learn to read. Teachers are quitting and parents are alarmed.

It's a mistake to see the system as some huge, monolithic object.

Like any human system, it's made up of individuals. Teachers, as individuals, feel isolated within the system. Like all of us, they are doing the best they possibly can. I have never met a teacher who did not want students to perform well and feel good about themselves. Many teachers are distressed by the failure of a student about whom they care deeply – but they lack the skills to help the student overcome the failure.

THE COGS IN THE WHEEL

By failure of the system, do we mean that teachers lack the necessary skills to produce efficient and effective learning in each of their students? Do we mean that teachers have been missing out on essential new information about learning and teaching and, out of ignorance, are doing harmful things? How does a teacher learn 'how' to teach?

How much does the teacher's personal experience as a student affect how they will teach? What room is there in the context of teaching for a teacher to continue to be a learner?

Students, as individuals, are part of the system too. A student's performance is an indication of a teacher's competence in the job. If they are not taught about the functioning of their brain and nervous system when they learn, it is because the adults in their environment don't know either. The result is that they are given very little room, permission or ability to say what is working for them and what is not. The system makes it easier to conform than to express – every day students witness the verbal, emotional and sometimes physical abuse heaped on students who try to express what's wrong for them. The theory behind the system is full of good intentions for students – but in reality, it shows little consideration for their world, their values, or their strengths.

And lastly, let's not forget that school administrations are made up of individuals too – individuals with impossible jobs. They run the system which brings teachers and students together in the classroom. They are faced with teacher shortages and growing class sizes. They hear that "the best are leaving," but they have to reconcile that with the fact that those who are leaving are no longer the best – so the best teacher can only be a teacher who stays. They are stuck between waring factions of parents, teachers, and students – all with different values. They are required to be teachers, learning experts, counsellors, politicians, negotiators and therapists. Everyone is important in the system – but the fastest changes will come from the teachers.

INDIVIDUAL SUCCESSES

If I give a student new strategies for learning which produce good results for that student, then I have helped one person. But one single child producing excellent results will not affect the system. Many students produce excellent results, but the system is not designed to look at how an outstanding student is producing those results so they can be generalised and passed on to others.

The only exception might be if I turn a student who is failing into a successful one. The student will, hopefully, be noticed and may change the attitude of a teacher or two. But my experience is that the student's new approach to learning will be belittled no matter how high the quality of the outcome. It's as if once pigeon-holed, forever pigeon-holed. And the student will need other personal skills to survive the heat they often have to take during this transition. They are told "See – I knew you had it in you," implying that the student previously had been slack. Worse still, some are confronted with aggression – they are asked "Who do you think you are?" – as if their success was a real threat to their teachers or their parents.

It is important to give new strategies to those who are strong enough to fight the system, and who will go onto use those strategies whether the system changes or not.

POWER POINTS

Administrators who become aware of what is possible with the new knowledge about learning can be powerful proponents of change. They can be instigators and sources of inspiration – but they may lack the skills to teach their teachers new methods; they may inadvertently attack teachers own ideas about their competence by suggesting this new way is the best way and thereby implying that what the teacher has been doing is wrong. Teachers can easily accuse administrators of not understanding the situation because they are not in the classroom every day; it is easy to disparage what they have to say about teaching.

Administrators are essential for change, but they are not at the point of real power – the power is with the teachers.

Individual teachers are the key to the whole game. A single teacher armed with strategies to reach every student in the class will change the game of learning for that student – perhaps forever. I have seen it time and time again – a single teacher believes in a student; a single teacher takes the time to give one student effective learning strategies; a single teacher doesn't judge the student as lazy, as stupid, as uninterested, but believes that if teaching is made to fit the student's learning style and talents, then the student can and will succeed. A single teacher can make a crucial difference in the entire life of a student.

TRUE BELIEVERS

Every successful person I have worked with has a story about a single individual who believed in them, and this person was almost always a teacher. That teacher stands out after many years as a primary influence in their lives – as someone who showed what really mattered; someone who showed them the other side of their weaknesses;

someone who believed that anything was possible for them and gave them their first taste of success.

An incompetent teacher can do damage but the influence of a hundred bad teachers can be undone, almost overnight, by a single good one. My mission is to make it possible for every student to have one such teacher – the teacher who will make the difference, the teacher who will be remembered forever.

I have worked with hundreds of teachers and more attend my programs every month. I stay in close contact with these groups. They have been willing to go back and remember what it was like to be in the classroom – to learn about learning styles and new approaches to teaching. They have been willing to learn about themselves and to stretch far beyond their personal comfort zones to learn new behaviours which change the whole dynamic of their classroom work.

It only takes one teacher to inspire hundreds of children. Teachers are the point of power.

I have learned many things about learning, and one belief (more than any other) comes to mind when I think of 'the system.' Where I direct my curiosity and attention leads to learning. I can always find what I'm looking for. If I focus on how the relationship between student X and teacher Y produced the result of student X not learning to read, I will learn how to reproduce that result in other students.

If I focus on how teacher Y produces reading ability in student X, then I will learn how to teach a student with the same learning style as student X, how to read. No more, no less. Teaching is less about teaching and more about learning.

If I examine how a teacher changes the study behaviour of a student to change consistently low marks to consistently high marks, then I will learn useful strategies for other failing students.

If I can find out how an F student goes on to change the world, and some have, then I will have some really useful strategies for F students. And those strategies won't be about how to get As – they'll be about how to be an F student and change the world.

If I study how a child who has acquired the dyslexia label grows up to be the head of a big company and leads a successful life, then I can discover things for others who carry the label.

I have chosen to focus my attention on how things work in the learning process.

- How do some teachers reach their students?
- How do some students go on to successful academic careers after having been labelled stupid by some parent or teacher?
- How did the un-coordinated meathead who sat in front of me in the 5th grade go on to be a professional athlete?
- How is it that some individuals do so well in the same failing system many people want to tear down and replace?
- How is it that the system is working at all?

If I can learn how the system does well, then I believe fast, effective, timely change can take place.

TEACHER BASHING HAS A PRICE

Many people who survived or even thrived in school, do to teachers exactly what teachers are accused of doing to their students. We tell teachers they're incompetent, they're lazy, they don't listen, they don't know what they're doing. How do you think they feel? What is the effect on teachers of this continuously reiterated message – on those we charge with our children's development? The same, I expect, as it is on anyone. Have you ever been harassed by your boss and gone home to harass your spouse? Many teachers expend incredible amounts of energy, they work hard day in and day out, knowing their own capacities and limitations, and then come home exhausted to read in the newspaper about what a terrible job they're doing. They feel just like the little kids who are also doing the best they can, ending a hard week with a failing grade and being told they are lazy, they don't listen, they have it easy, will have to be punished, are no good and pretty stupid to boot.

If teachers and the system they have to work in, are continually bashed with accusations and threats, adverse consequences are inevitable. Teacher bashers need to stop and think – just for a moment. I'd like to see them try to survive a week in a room full of teenagers.

It is important to remember that teachers are themselves products of the same system. I hear, far too often, the generalisation that teachers should know. Know what? How should they know? Their knowledge of teaching is based primarily on their own experience in school and on what they learned in college, where they repeat the same patterns, even when they don't work. If the system doesn't teach them how to teach effectively, how can we justify bashing them when we think they don't do the job? But despite all the negativity, some teachers go on to work miracles in the classrooms. I want to know how they do that.

LOSING THE GOOD

The loss of good teachers is our single greatest threat. For every qualified teacher who leaves the system, hundreds of children – our future leaders and workers – might be denied the future they deserve.

The first and most significant problem facing the education system is lack of respect for teachers. Teachers have been forced into such an entrenched, defensive position, that few will welcome change if it is presented as a forcible remedy for what outsiders perceive as their failure. My guiding principle when I work with teachers is that they are doing the best they know how.

TEACHERS ARE NOT THE ENEMY

What do teachers want? Most teachers I meet take their job seriously; they want to feel good about what they've accomplished at the end of a day; they like the high when a student learns something; they like to learn themselves; they work long hours; they feel responsible for the future of Australia's next generations; they respond like most of us to positive reinforcement; they want to make a difference. And then they read newspapers telling them how poorly they are doing their jobs.

TEACHERS MAKE GREAT STUDENTS

Teachers are the single most responsive group I have trained. They have surprised me with how much they already know – how many new thoughts they are attempting to put to work. They want to succeed, and to them, success is how much and how well their students learn. Teachers I work with, no matter how fearful of change they might be in the beginning, respond just like anyone else. Everyone loves to be right. Everyone loves to be productive. Everyone loves to do a good job.

The most encouraging words I hear from teachers is that they've learned a few new things that might be the difference that makes a difference – and they're going to stick with teaching to see if they can

Stephanie Burns

make it all work. The most discouraging words were "I've been doing this for 15 years and this is my last year – I want to get out before the stigma 'teacher' is attached for good."

What is it that teachers are doing well? For one thing, they get up every morning and do what most of us pray never to have a nightmare about. They do the best they know how in extreme situations, knowing they don't have the time or the resources to reach everyone. They use short cuts to make it the best day they can.

THE BLACKBOARD JUNGLE

When does a teacher become ineffective? Even though teachers in fact hold the power, the prevailing lack of respect for them in the community means they cannot openly influence the system, and the old guard, with the new information they are learning. Those teachers who do succeed in influencing the system do so because their school possesses an open-minded administrator.

Teachers who don't have that blessing have to resort to covert operations – uncover warfare. Some are brilliant at it; they should get medals for the risks they take and for the courage and conviction they are dedicating to the future of this country. But, sadly, they can do little to change the system.

Some teachers run into trouble because they try to sell new ideas with words and concepts, instead of just doing it, and letting the results speak for themselves.

A lack of access to education in the neurosciences means they don't understand the need to stimulate the brain and the nervous system to produce good patterning in their students.

Through a lack of education in learning strategies, they are allowing students to fail in areas where failing is actually very difficult to do.

Through a lack of awareness of the brain and body as a learning system, they work against natural propensities to learn, to change, to grow and to adapt.

Teachers are both right and wrong. They do their best with the experience and the equipment they have. They know they need new choices. If every student isn't performing to maximum potential, then teachers know they need to learn more about teaching.

THE "SO WHATs"

I have spent most of my life looking for the things that really matter, and in the process, I've had to confront the endless dreary, unthinking ravings in the media about things that in the end don't matter.

A Bad Teacher is a "So What"

It's not what happens, it's what you do about what happens. If what happens really mattered, then no one who had a teacher who made us feel worthless would have survived – and most of us can name at least one.

To me, that bad teacher is a "so what" – a non-essential. It's not what happened, it's what I did – I decided that teacher was a jerk.

Good Nutrition is a "So What"

A healthy body responds better in a learning situation – I agree. However, it is a "so what." It's a help if you have it, but if you don't, and you can find a hundred examples of malnourished kids who turned into powerful, successful adults, then it is a "so what". Nice, but still not essential.

A Happy Home Life is a "So What"

Again, nice if you've got it, great if you can teach people to have it, but once more, there are too many models of success from lousy homes. Nice, but not essential.

Recently, amazing stories have surfaced of illiterate adults coming out of the closet. Some of them never got past their illiteracy, but many used other strategies to move on to success. Their inability to read didn't stand in the way.

Having a Learning Disability is a "So What"

First of all, based on my experiences with people who carry these labels, I find few that fit the category.

Most merely did some quite natural things that were too quickly evaluated as a problem. The problem got lots of attention and they learned to generalise it into everything they did.

The labelling of students as learning disabled is one of the single most devastating things to occur in schools in recent history.

Read the latest Who's Who. Many successful people tell stories of learning difficulties. In fact, if statistics say anything, the student labelled as learning disabled stands a better chance of a successful life than the so-called "normal" student. If you've been labelled like this, stand up and cheer – you're in very good company.

IT IS NOT THAT THESE AREN'T IMPORTANT ISSUES

I am saying that if you can categorise them as "so what," you can then move on to "What am I going to do about it?" From there, you can get somewhere.

Let's face it – if we wait until every kid has a good home, good food, we've moved past the negative labelling of students and all teachers are great, we'd have seen pigs fly first.

These factors and hundreds of others that occupy the "concerned" part of people's minds are important; making things better for all children should always be a high priority.

But with school and learning, we are dealing with now – with today. And these issues, although important, must not be allowed to obscure the undeniable fact that they are not obstacles to genuine success in life.

THE 'SHOULDS'

"Shoulds" are another area of misplaced attention. I hear so much about how schools "should" look, how students "should" behave, what they "should" watch, read or wear. But for every "should" there are hundreds of exceptions.

LOOKING FOR WHAT MATTERS

The essential things, the things that matter in a successful life, must be learned somewhere along the way. I believe this should be in school, which then will play a more significant role than it does today. I have looked for the differences that make a difference. If the teacher is educated about learning, about the brain and the nervous system, about beliefs and values, about motivation, change and stimulation, about framing experiences in useful ways, about talent, desire, optimism, then conditions are almost irrelevant – a school set up in a garage with cement floors, 40degree heat and students from every conceivable background will produce good results. It's being done all over the world.

If what these newly educated teachers have learned is passed on to their students, then no matter how good or bad the teacher may be, their students will learn and succeed.

These are the skills I discuss in this book. I didn't make them up. I have been a highly effective teacher, trainer and lecturer because I have identified what works and then taught others to use the same good strategies. I have examined what I have done, preserved the good and discarded the bad; I have examined what others do, sometimes much better than I can. And as I applied what I learned, I constantly modified it in the light of feedback from my students.

AND IN THE END

Nearing the end of Sunday night, it's coming to the close of the Learning To Learn weekend seminar I conduct and the students gather around the stage. As they settle into place, their faces evoke funny and sometimes touching stories about the experiences I've had over the weekend. This is a slice of the human race.

Some are doctors, some are truck drivers, students, parents, some are 13 years old, some are retired and turning 70. Some have a college degree, some dropped out of school at 15. Some love to read, and some have read more in the last two days than in the last ten years. Some are pessimists for whom most learning situations were difficult. Some had been labelled learning disabled, and some came with the belief they suffered from dyslexia. Some are optimists. Some are teachers, some want to be, and some wouldn't dream of it. Some are successful but feel they'll never amount to much. Some are people who seem to glide through life singing songs out loud in the car. A psychologist and a street kid sit next to each other, and in another spot a professional clown and a nurse.

These are the people I work with and for; no two are the same. What one has learned to do with ease another will struggle to accomplish. When one laughs out loud, another is embarrassed. Where one says, "I'll give it a go", another says, "Do I have to?"

Some tell me they loved school and wish they were back there. Others are merely glad they survived the experience intact. Some are back to class early to tidy their materials, others never open a notebook. Someone gets 20 per cent on my vocabulary test and is a voracious reader: another gets 90 per cent and prefers to listen to music.

They are all different, but with one experience in common. They are all products of the education system.

DIFFERENCES THAT MAKE A DIFFERENCE

This book has been about the differences that make a difference for those who have survived or thrived in the traditional education system.

On this Sunday night, looking at my students, what amazes me most is that I don't know who's who. I don't know who is the clown and who is the doctor. To me, they are people with the common goal of learning more effectively. To me, they all look the same.

The seventy, one hundred, or even two hundred people I face at the end of the Learning To Learn, have all spent a weekend discovering that with excellent teaching they become excellent learners. With an understanding of the learning process, they become their own excellent teachers.

They have learned that anything is possible. For one weekend, they have had an opportunity to explore their own best way of doing things; they learned new choices which will stay with them the next time they sit to read, or write, or run around the block, or talk to their children.

They have come to terms with the fact that their actions produce consequences and that they can change the consequences by changing their actions. They all exhibit the same skills through the diversity of their learning styles.

They have, often for the first time in their lives, experienced an environment that unconditionally believes that they are doing the best they know how, so far. They have been respected as a human being whose divine right is to be able to learn.

At this time in my weekend training, the students would all say the weekend was about something different. Each of them had their own dragons to fight and battles to win. Some were 'belief' dragons, and some 'attitude' dragons, and some 'I never knew that about my brain!' dragons. Some have learned to interpret events in more useful ways. Some learned to jump in and try things out first. Some learned about the effect of their physiology on their brain and subsequently on their state of mind. Some learned that they have been okay since the beginning and their second grade teacher who said, "You're stupid and will never amount to anything" really didn't know what she was talking about.

YOU CAN BE YOU

Participants in the Learning To Learn weekend training undergo many direct experiences of what is possible for them; they learn that all good strategies for learning are commonsense, easy. We were designed to learn – naturally and efficiently.

They come to terms with the fact that it's all been there all the time, if only they had looked, or had someone pointed them in the right direction.

At the end of the weekend I ask one very simple, yet profound question: "Based on the evidence you have seen of your own performance and improvements during even one day here, if you were to improve by that same amount in any area of endeavour you chose, every day for one year who could you be?"

They use examples to describe their personal dreams. I have been told, "I could do what Buckminster Fuller has done." "I could be Leonardo daVinci." "I could acquire the skills to change the world." "I could go back to school." "I could be a great teacher." Sometimes – the most profound – "I can be more of me, I can be anything."

THE TRANSITION

Simply because we come to some new understanding, about beliefs on performance, for example, it takes time to acquire new skills based on that information. No one has done it before, it takes re-patterning and it takes the experience of many people playing around for many years to finally say, "There, that's how you learn effectively."

In the end, as with every endeavour, it will be about what the Learning To Learn graduate does with the lessons of the weekend. Many will go on to fulfil a personal dream while others will be the support for someone else to achieve their goal. Some may do nothing. Maybe a few will go on to change the world for the better. And that is my reward.